ON
VIRTUES

ON VIRTUES

U. S. SENATOR SHELDON WHITEHOUSE

QUOTATIONS AND INSIGHT
TO LIVE A FULL, HONORABLE,
AND
Truly AMERICAN *Life*

A **adams**media

Avon, Massachusetts

Published by
Adams Media, a division of F+W Media, Inc.
57 Littlefield Street, Avon, MA 02322. U.S.A.
www.adamsmedia.com

ISBN 10: 1-4405-3876-X
ISBN 13: 978-1-4405-3876-6
eISBN 10: 1-4405-5127-8
eISBN 13: 978-1-4405-5127-7

Printed in the United States of America.

10   9   8   7   6   5   4   3   2   1

Library of Congress Cataloging-in-Publication Data
Whitehouse, Sheldon.
On virtues / by Sheldon Whitehouse.
p. cm.
ISBN 978-1-4405-3876-6 (hardcover : alk. paper) – ISBN 1-4405-3876-X (hardcover
: alk. paper) – ISBN 978-1-4405-5127-7 (ebook : alk. paper) – ISBN 1-4405-5127-8
(ebook : alk. paper)
1. Conduct of life—Quotations, maxims, etc. I. Title.
BJ1521.W45 2012
179'.9—dc23
2012019349

This book is available at quantity discounts for bulk purchases.
For information, please call 1-800-289-0963.

CONTENTS

INTRODUCTION

My family was a foreign service family. As I was growing up, my father was posted to Cambodia, South Africa, Congo, Guinea, Vietnam, Laos, and Thailand, with stints in New York City at the United Nations and Washington, D.C., at the State Department. Some of the foreign postings were pretty primitive and unpleasant. Some of the nations were at war.

My father's service made for an interesting childhood. His assignments meant a lot of time for me in boarding school, and an early start on independence. But they also sent a powerful silent message: *something* was worth it. Something was worth my mom's having to worry about not having a decent hospital nearby when I broke my arm, or worry about how we'd get the rabies vaccine when my brother got bitten by a street dog (a friend's mother died of rabies, so this was not an idle worry). Something was worth not being able to drink the water safely. Something was worth the family separations that safety and schooling demanded.

That something is a big part of what this book of quotations is about. I have gathered them in a little handwritten notebook, bit by bit, over nearly twenty years, as I came across words and phrases that touched on that something.

In my family we never talked about what that something was. It was like a dark star—you only knew it was there by its effect on other things. Perhaps that something was too big to talk about.

Perhaps that's why I find it easier to look for that something in other people's words than to describe it in my own.

I can tell you this. That something has a lot to do with America and what America stands for: with our system of government, and its balance and counterpoise; with our belief in principles above power; with our American sense of journey; with what we mean in the world. It has a lot to do with the rule of law, and to a degree, with the craft of lawyering that brings the rule of law to life. It has a lot to do with the little glimpses into the eternal that adherence to principle provides. And it has a lot to do with the difficulties, frustrations, and defeats that are the virtually inevitable price of working hands-on in our government of laws, and with the political combat that shapes and drives our government and its laws.

And, truth be told, a bit of this book is just picked from the clutter of my own experiences: snippets of poetry and prayer and phrase that seemed particularly telling, evocative or resonant—even some that are just plain silly, since life can be pretty silly sometimes.

Working on this collection has brought back a flood of memories of that early life, and of my father. The earliest memory is sitting at my breakfast table on a sunny morning, I think in Cambodia, looking across the room at my father at a different breakfast table having a different breakfast, reading his newspaper. My time with him was in the evening, when he came home from the embassy, and made his ritual cocktail-hour martini. (This was a lifelong practice, culminating at the end when he took himself off the hated chemo and announced, "Enough of that damned stuff, I'm going to treat this with a martini.") For me, he stirred together cold milk and a black-currant syrup called Ribena in my little cup. To this day, I still love the taste of black currant, and enjoy the happy sound of a cocktail shaker. We would have our drinks together, before I was shuffled off to bed and he and my mother settled down to dinner.

I remember the incomplete and uncertain feeling of our first Christmas without him. He'd been sent to the Congo during the Lumumba Rebellion, and it was dangerous enough there that no family members were allowed. That left my mother and my little brother and me to have Christmas together. My mother tried so hard to make it cheerful that I felt I had to try hard, too, not to let her down. I think I was six.

I remember the unaccustomed sight of my father in the kitchen in our house in Conakry, Guinea. It was afternoon, when the household staff (all spies of the Guinean government) were away. He had bags of groceries from the embassy commissary spread out around the kitchen counters, and was hiding walkie-talkies inside bread loaves to deliver to the embassy families. We had all been put under house arrest by the Guinean government. My father had negotiated permission to deliver groceries to the imprisoned families, and this was how he was going to make sure that everyone could communicate, and how he was going to know that everyone was all right—that nothing awful was happening. Off he went, with our embassy Wagoneer stuffed with grocery bags and secrets, leaving a son amazed at his father's capacity for such an intrigue, proud to be in on the secret. I was probably ten.

I think back now, as a parent with the daily worries of life, to my mother, with two boys oblivious to the dangers and cheerfully ready for mischief, and a baby daughter to look after. Get bitten by the wrong dog and it's rabies; drink the wrong water and it's parasites; swim in the wrong creek and it's bilharzia; fall off your bike in the wrong gutter and it's infection from the sewage: no milk, no hospital, sporadic electricity—not a mother's dream posting. And we children gave her plenty more to worry about. During a particularly angry demonstration against America and "neocolonialism," my little brother Charlie and I climbed up on the roof to get a better view of the crowds surging by either side of the house. Of course we did not tell my mother. All she knew was that suddenly we were nowhere to be found, my father was away at the embassy, and large angry mobs were protesting outside. By the time she found us on the roof, she was nearly as ready to kill us as she was relieved to find us. She scrambled me and Charlie over the wall into the next compound, occupied by a Saudi official, and instructed us in no uncertain terms to go inside his house and not budge until my father returned and picked us up. Charlie and I sat there in near silence, for hours, awkwardly perching on overly ornate furniture, chilly in an overly air-conditioned room, picking at an unfamiliar plate of nut candies the kind Saudi had put out, and contemplating our grim future.

The miseries and hazards of Conakry, Guinea, highlighted my father's particularly strong sense of duty. He had dated Jacqueline Bouvier. His sister Sylvia had been a bridesmaid in Jackie's wedding to John Fitzgerald Kennedy. Jacqueline Kennedy was now the First Lady and JFK was President. On their way through the snows from their Inaugural Ball, the new President and First Lady had made one stop, at the home of Susan Mary Alsop, my father's cousin. My father and the President were both Ivy League, combat-hardened, Pacific theater veterans. Were it not for the convention of calling him "Mr. President," he and the President likely would have been on a first-name basis. With one phone call, my father could probably have been out of Conakry. It simply was not in him to contemplate making such a call. "When duty calls, or danger, be never wanting there," was his lifelong motto.

* * *

America changed during my father's years in Vietnam, and so did we. He shipped out in 1968, to take over for the legendary John

Paul Vann (subject of the book, *A Bright and Shining Lie*) as the civilian commander of Military Region Three, around Saigon. Vann was assigned to the same position in MR Four, the Delta region, and was shortly after killed in action there. That brought a pretty keen sense of the danger of my father's job. He finally came back from Vietnam in 1973, after serving as deputy ambassador.

During that period, America had gone from Martin Luther King Jr.'s assassination through the resignation of President Nixon, with the My Lai massacre and the moon landing and Woodstock and Kent State and Watergate as mileposts along the way. Although my father saw us intermittently, on holidays, he came home to the United States rarely and briefly. (I lived with him in Saigon for several months—I think the only dependent in the history of the Vietnam conflict.) Upon his return a chasm had opened between us and the America we knew, and him and the America he had left. We took a family vacation to Walt Disney World, and my mother bought him new, bright-blue nylon Nike sneakers (in his world, sneakers were still white canvas, maybe with a blue stripe around the sole). He wore the Nikes once, and I ultimately grabbed them for myself. By then, we were the same shoe size.

The following year I took time off from school before college. I lived with my father at his new post in Laos, a heartbreakingly beautiful country, with lovely, kind people, into which our international contest with communism had violently intruded. The consequences for Laos were devastating. To my father fell the distasteful duty of negotiating America's departure and the establishment of a coalition government, which ultimately led to a communist takeover by the Pathet Lao, the murder of the royal family, and a national campaign of "reeducation" that decimated the Hmong people and sent waves of refugees into neighboring Thailand. America had lost interest in Southeast Asia, and Laos paid the price.

Years later, during my father's retirement, a Lao temple was proposed in nearby Virginia, provoking local opposition suspicious of the new arrivals. My father loved to tell the story of the night of the hearing, when he arrived to testify with his military aide and a CIA station chief from the Laos days. The CIA officer, Hugh Tovar, began his testimony, "The first encounter I had with the Lao people was when I parachuted at midnight into the Plain of Jars . . . ." Silence fell in the hearing room. General Richard Trefry, then the commander of White House military operations, and in full military regalia, testified that without the courageous Lao resistance there would be one thousand more names on the Vietnam War Memorial. My father then summed up, and when it was time for testimony in opposition, the crowd sat in silence. The temple was approved. I think he felt some small sense of personal atonement.

I don't say that because he ever said so; indeed it amazes me, still, the things we never talked about. When he was called out of retirement to the Pentagon to start Special Operations Command, the young SEAL and Delta Force officers on his staff decided to check out the old diplomat, and discovered that he was due a variety of military decorations including something like seventeen Air Medals from his World War II service in the U.S. Marine Corps. He'd never bothered to put in for them.

My uncle George Bruen Whitehouse was my father's younger brother and childhood soul mate. The two had also been children of a foreign service family. Friends, schoolmates, even schools, were scarce in faraway locations, so they were particularly close brothers. Fifty years later, when my father saw the restored sailboat that they had sailed together as boys on Narragansett Bay, he was overcome with emotion—the first and only time his children saw that in his life.

In World War II, Uncle George joined up after his freshman year at Yale and became a Navy fighter pilot, flying off the carrier USS *Cow-*

pens. On his first combat mission he was shot down over the Philippines. His body was never recovered. When my father lay dying, and I was helping him finish a memoir, we talked for the first time about his trip after the war to Legaspi in the Philippines to search for his brother's remains. You can imagine his sentiments on the long trip over, the anticipation of what he might find if he were successful, the frustration of walking through villages and down trails hoping someone might remember a plane that had crashed, the empty feeling on the long flight home. Yet only at the end did we discuss it, even briefly.

There were lessons from this foreign service childhood. I saw members of the Lao royal family at public events pretty frequently, and shortly afterward they were all dead. Our posting to South Africa was during the evil days of apartheid, around the time of the Sharpeville Massacre. One day my father came home from the State Department for dinner and announced that the last remaining Guinean official he'd worked with was gone—all dead or dungeoned at the hands of the tyrant Sékou Touré. I traveled into An Lôc with my father shortly after its recapture and every building was pitted with bullet and shrapnel holes, every home and store empty. Whatever dangers or discomforts we faced paled in comparison to the violence, disease, and poverty around us in these posts. We had a window on the danger, close up, and sometimes it could creep through that window (as it did for my friend's mother who contracted and died of rabies), but we were not condemned to it. For us, there was always America, and home, to come back to.

* * *

Our human species is capable of lying and theft, of plunder and massacre, of doubt and folly. We are often wicked to one another, and greedy. Yet out of these feet of clay, from time to time, we rise to courage and wisdom and honor and sacrifice that touch the divine. We capture these occasions with words, and we save and remember those words, to be inspired again.

Our governance of one another, across the span of history, has often been little more than the organized application of our human species' worst tendencies. But into that world came our American system of government. Our American system of government balanced those evil tendencies, and set them against each other, and created sanctuaries from them. Within our system of government, the effects of those worst tendencies are muted, or delayed while passions cool, or directed around safe havens that shelter us. This remarkable, resilient set of interlocking balances was crafted in words—in the words of our Constitution and Bill of Rights. Those words remain our country's compass.

Words matter. Nathan Hale would be just another dead man at the end of a rope, bones moldered into decay, name lost to oblivion —except that before that rope snapped taut against his neck, he said, "I only regret that I have but one life to lose for my country." In that one breath of words, he stepped into history. Ronald Reagan captured the long precipice tread to victory in the Cold War when he told Mikhail Gorbachev in four unforgettable words, "Tear down this wall." Martin Luther King Jr.'s words on the National Mall made his dream of racial reconciliation real for millions of Americans, and his words echo still through the decades. Words matter.

I have had the chance to see our government from many angles: as a child in a foreign service family, and as an adult with a family of my own; as a lowly clerk in the judicial branch, and advocating before the highest court in the land; working for the federal government, and serving my home state of Rhode Island. I have held office in the executive and legislative branches; been a principal and a staffer; served in very political roles and completely apolitical ones; worked in times of calm and plenty, and times of distress and discord. I've been an active campaigner in political contests and I have patiently constructed complex governmental reforms.

I began to collect these words to help me in those roles and tasks, as a reference for myself, to help me grow wiser and more effective. As my children came of age, I came to realize that the collection was also for them. Whether they grow up to serve as citizens or senators, two offices happily equal in our American system, I hope these words connect them to that something, which we still don't speak of, but which has been so important a force in my life.

This book is dedicated to them and to my wife, Sandra. Bill Clinton once told me that I was one of the most "overmarried" men he'd ever seen. He's right. Sandra is the love of my life, and I don't know what I'd have done without her.

My father, mother, brother, and me.

CHAPTER ONE

COURAGE, CONSCIENCE, AND CONVICTION

To know what is right and not to do it is
the worst form of cowardice.

—CONFUCIUS

And the Lord said, whom shall I send, and who shall go for us? Then said I, here am I; send me.

—ISAIAH 6:8

I used this quote in my father's eulogy. It captured well his lifetime of service. On his wall at home hung a framed dagger, given him at the end of his service at Special Operations Command, whose plaque was inscribed with these words.

I am aware that many object to the severity of my language, but is there not cause for severity? I will be as harsh as truth, and as uncompromising as justice. On this subject, I do not wish to think, or speak, or write, with moderation. No! No! Tell a man whose house is on fire to give a moderate alarm; tell him to moderately rescue his wife from the hands of the ravisher; tell the mother to gradually extricate her babe from the fire into which it has fallen;—but urge me not to use moderation in a cause like the present. I am in earnest—I will not equivocate—I will not excuse—I will not retreat a single inch—and I will be heard!

—WILLIAM LLOYD GARRISON, STATEMENT OF EDITORIAL POLICY OF THE ANTISLAVERY *LIBERATOR*, JANUARY 1831

A fine paean to the occasional need for immoderation.

Inconsistencies of opinion arising from changes of circumstance are often justifiable. But there is one sort of inconsistency that is culpable: it is the inconsistency between a man's conviction and his vote, between his conscience and his conduct.
—DANIEL WEBSTER, QUOTED IN *PROFILES IN COURAGE*

In his speech on the Munich Agreement, Churchill condemned those who "court political popularity," and praised "that firmness of character which is utterly unmoved by currents of opinion, however swift and violent they may be."

*   *   *

To serve the Publick faithfully, and at the same time please it entirely, is impracticable.
—BENJAMIN FRANKLIN, FROM
POOR RICHARD'S ALMANAC, 1758

Your representative owes you, not his industry only, but his judgment; and he betrays, instead of serving you, if he sacrifices it to your opinion.
—EDMUND BURKE

Government provides many opportunities for the application of these statements, for better or for worse. Swift and violent currents of opinion may later leave a tidewrack of regret, but I have seen good people yield to them.

And when the strife

Is fierce, the warfare long,

Steals on the ear

The distant triumph song,

And hearts are brave

Again, and arms are strong

Alleluia! Alleluia!

—HYMN: "FOR ALL THE SAINTS," WILLIAM HOW

A beautiful hymn, to a soaring, singable tune, riddled with beautiful phrases, but none more beautiful than this last stanza and its final "Alleluias." We carried my father's casket out of the church to this hymn.

G reat ideals are the glory of man alone. No other creature can have them. Only man can get a vision and an inspiration that will lift him above the level of himself and send him forth against all opposition or any discouragement to do and to dare and to accomplish wonderful and great things for the world and for humanity.

—MATTHEW HENSON, THE AFRICAN AMERICAN POLAR EXPLORER ON THE PEARY EXPEDITION TO THE NORTH POLE IN 1909

A great expression of man's gift for courage and conviction. Henson was, because Peary became incapacitated, probably the first man to set foot on the North Pole.

Real courage is . . . when you know you're licked before you begin but you begin anyway and you see it through no matter what. You rarely win, but sometimes you do.

—HARPER LEE'S *TO KILL A MOCKINGBIRD*

To Kill a Mockingbird *honors the lonely nature of courage and conscience through these words of its hero Atticus Finch, as well as in his observation, "The only thing that doesn't abide by majority rule is a person's conscience." Not all courage is honored by everyone: at the end of the trial, Atticus is packing up his papers in an empty courtroom. But the gallery has remained, and as Atticus walks out, the elderly preacher tells Atticus's daughter, Scout, "Stand up. Your father's passing."*

* * *

I would say that a first-rate man is one—is a man that did the best he could with what talents he had to make something which wasn't here yesterday . . . that [he] never hurt an inferior, never harmed the weak, practiced honesty and courtesy, and tried to be as brave as he wanted to be whether he always was that brave or not.

—WILLIAM FAULKNER, FROM "FAULKNER AT VIRGINIA"

It's not easy to be brave, and trying counts for a lot.

No captain can do very wrong if he places his ship alongside that of the enemy.

No maneuvers. Go right at them.

—BOTH BY LORD NELSON, AS CITED BY PATRICK O'BRIAN'S WONDERFUL CHARACTER JACK AUBREY

Two good and authoritative recommendations of the direct approach. Obviously, the purpose of placing your ship alongside that of the enemy is to exchange broadsides, the most violent and destructive means of military combat of that era, naval or land. But as documented in Nelson Speaks, his rationale was thus: "Not a moment should be lost in attacking the enemy. . . . The only consideration in my mind is, how to get at them with the least risk to our ships. . . . The measure may be thought bold, but I am of the opinion the boldest measures are the safest." A similar expression of boldness in naval engagements is by Captain John Paul Jones, which appears on the Navy Memorial near my apartment in Washington: "I wish to have no connection with any ship that does not sail fast; for I intend to go in harm's way."

Do you know what's shown on board of the Commander-in-Chief? Why, [the signal] to leave off action! Now damn me if I do! You know, Foley, I have only one eye,—I have a right to be blind sometimes. I really do not see the signal!

——HORATIO NELSON

Admiral Lord Nelson in a great sea battle (the Battle of Copenhagen, 1801) ignored a signal commanding him to disengage with the enemy. (Admiral Byng's hanging, made famous by Voltaire's remark that "every once in a while you have to hang an admiral to encourage all the others," showed how perilous this decision was.) Informed of the order from the flagship, Nelson put his telescope to his blind eye (previously lost at the Siege of Calvi). His decision won the day for the British Navy. This is a favorite story. I tell it to kids whenever I can. Courage, daring, rule-breaking and vindication, all rolled into one. What could be better! Sometimes you must put the telescope to your blind eye.

Men Wanted: for Hazardous Journey. Small wages, bitter cold, long months of complete darkness, constant danger, safe return doubtful. Honor and recognition in case of success.

——SIR ERNEST SHACKLETON'S ALLEGED ADVERTISEMENT

Shackleton was a great self-promoter, and there may have been an element of theater in this advertisement for his polar expedition. But men did respond—and think what those responses say about them!

L abour to keep alive in your breast that little spark of celestial fire called conscience.

—GEORGE WASHINGTON'S "RULES OF CIVILITY AND DECENT BEHAVIOUR"

George Washington, like most of the great men of the Revolutionary era, was self-conscious about his public image, to the extent of keeping a little book of rules to guide his public behavior. Many involve deportment, protocol, and hygiene. This one stands apart. It was the final one, number 110.

We would not die in that man's company
That fears his fellowship to die with us.
This day is called the Feast of Crispian:
He that outlives this day, and comes safe home,
Will stand a-tiptoe when this day is nam'd,
And rouse him at the name of Crispian.
He that shall see this day, and live old age,
Will yearly on the vigil feast his neighbors,
And say, "Tomorrow is Saint Crispian."
Then will he strip his sleeve and show his scars,
And say, "These wounds I had on Crispin's day."
Old men forget; yet all shall be forgot,
But he'll remember, with advantages,
What feats he did that day. Then shall our names,
Familiar in his mouth as household words,
Harry the King, Bedford and Exeter,
Warwick and Talbot, Salisbury and Gloucester,
Be in their flowing cups freshly remember'd.

This story shall the good man teach his son;
And Crispin Crispian shall ne'er go by,
From this day to the ending of the world,
But we in it shall be remembered:
We few, we happy few, we band of brothers;
For he to-day that sheds his blood with me
Shall be my brother; be he ne'er so vile,
This day shall gentle his condition.
And gentlemen in England, now a-bed,
Shall think themselves accursed they were not here,
And hold their manhoods cheap whiles any speaks
That fought with us upon Saint Crispin's day.
—SHAKESPEARE, *HENRY V*, ACT 4, SCENE 3

At the ensuing battle at Agincourt in 1415, the outnumbered English slaughtered a vastly superior French army by the thousands in a field of mud. There is no better expression of underdog esprit de corps than Shakespeare's "we few, we happy few, we band of brothers."

Upon this battle depends the
  survival of Christian civilization.

Upon it depends our own British life
  and the long continuity of our
    institutions, and our Empire.

The whole fury and might of the enemy
  must very soon be turned upon us.

Hitler knows that he will have to break
  us in this island, or lose the war.

If we can stand up to him,
  all Europe may be freed,
    and the life of the world
      may move forward into
        broad and sunlit uplands.

But if we fail,
  then the whole world,
    including the United States,
      and all that we have known and
          cared for,

will sink into the abyss of a
　　new Dark Age
　　　made more sinister and
　　　　perhaps more prolonged by
　　　　the lights of perverted
　　　　　science.

Let us therefore brace ourselves to
　our duties, and so bear ourselves that
　　if the British Empire and
　　　Commonwealth last for a
　　　　thousand years, men will still
　　　　　say,
　　　　　　"This was their finest hour."

　　　　　——WINSTON CHURCHILL

There is so much to love about this speech, reproduced here in the style Churchill liked for delivery: the epic cost of the stakes; the simple words; the familiar Churchillisms like "broad and sunlit uplands"; and the gathering windup in the penultimate paragraph leading to the glorious closing line, "This was their finest hour." No closing line was ever better set up. And beyond the rhetoric lies the stark reality that Churchill could then say and believe, that upon this battle depended the survival of Christian civilization, and British life, institutions, and Empire.

Through our great good fortune, in our youth our hearts were touched with fire. It was given to us to learn at the outset that life is a profound and passionate thing. While we are permitted to scorn nothing but indifference, and do not pretend to undervalue the worldly rewards of ambition, we have seen with our own eyes, beyond and above the gold fields the snowy heights of honor, and it is for us to bear the report to those who come after us. But above all, we have learned that whether a man accepts from Fortune her spade, and will look downward and dig, or from Aspiration her axe and cord, and will scale the ice, the one and only success which it is his to command, is to bring to his work a mighty heart.

—Oliver Wendell Holmes Jr., on his
generation's experiences with the Civil War

This paragraph is shot through with elegant phrases, but the best of all Holmes's observations is his reminder that the one and only success that is always ours to command is to bring to our work a mighty heart. Holmes has also said more prosaically, "Every calling is great when greatly pursued."

There is only one power, conscience in the service of justice; and there is only one glory, genius in the service of truth.

—VICTOR HUGO, IN HIS ORATION HONORING VOLTAIRE

I'm drawn in this quote to the phrase "conscience in the service of justice"—at once workmanlike and inspiring.

Mine eyes have seen the glory of the coming of the Lord;

He is trampling out the vintage where the grapes of wrath
are stored;

He hath loosed the fateful lightning of His terrible swift
sword:

His truth is marching on.

Glory! Glory! Hallelujah! His truth is marching on.

I have seen Him in the watch fires of a hundred circling
camps;

They have builded Him an altar in the evening dews and
damps;

I can read His righteous sentence in the dim and flaring
lamps;

His day is marching on!

In the beauty of the lilies Christ was born across the sea,

With a glory in His bosom that transfigures you and me;

As He died to make men holy, let us die to make men free;

While God is marching on!

——Hymn: "Battle Hymn of the Republic,"
Julia Ward Howe

"Let us die to make men free." And they did——Union casualties in the Civil War numbered approximately 360,000, from a Northern population numbering around 22 million. The equivalent number of causalities for today's American population would be around 5 million.

A proper resignation to the will of the Divine Being is the certain foundation for true bravery.

—WILLIAM DIGBY, BRITISH SOLDIER IN THE REVOLUTIONARY WAR QUOTED BY RICHARD M. KETCHUM IN *SARATOGA*.

This seems a very good way to connect faith and courage. Someone who has experienced more danger than I have would know better.

Courage is like love. It must have hope to nourish it.
—NAPOLEON BONAPARTE, QUOTED IN JOHN McCAIN'S
BOOK *WHY COURAGE MATTERS*

Senator John McCain's use of this quote in his book adds emphasis to it. He is the man I know who most demonstrably knows something about courage.

* * *

¡Sí se puede!
—CESAR CHAVEZ

"Yes, it can be done." Cesar Chavez had nothing, and represented people who had nothing, and threw himself into opposition with the most powerful interests of his time and place. He prevailed with the simple resolute courage embodied by this phrase, which became his motto. My friend George Nee, a great Rhode Island labor leader, was his bodyguard during these struggles.

I t was accomplished by a display of courage that only escaped foolhardiness by virtue of the skill with which it was performed.

—INSURER'S DESCRIPTION OF A SALVAGE RESCUE IN
FARLEY MOWAT'S *THE GREY SEAS UNDER*

The Grey Seas Under *is one of the great books ever written about men and the sea. Buried within it is this beautifully spare and elegant language taken from a marine insurance adjuster's report about a salvage endeavored by the gallant rescue tug.*

Let us, then, be up and doing,
With a heart for any fate;
Still achieving, still pursuing,
Learn to labor and to wait.

—HENRY WADSWORTH LONGFELLOW,
"A PSALM OF LIFE"

These were the final words of the Senate eulogy to Edward Kennedy delivered by his longtime friend and often rival, Robert C. Byrd, after forty-seven years of service together in the Senate.

CHAPTER TWO

DILIGENCE, DUTY, AND DETERMINATION

Hard work overcomes everything.

—VIRGIL, THE *GEORGICS*

It little profits that an idle king,
By this still hearth, among these barren crags,
Matched with an aged wife, I mete and dole
Unequal laws unto a savage race,
That hoard and sleep, and feed and know not me.
. . . .
Come, my friends,
'Tis not too late to seek a newer world.
. . . .
Tho' much is taken, much abides; and tho'
We are not now that strength which in old days
Moved earth and heaven, that which we are, we are;
One equal temper of heroic hearts,
Made weak by time and fate, but strong in will
To strive, to seek, to find, and not to yield.
—Alfred Lord Tennyson, "Ulysses"

I love this poem. Life wears on us: "much is taken." Yet the powerful energy of a determined and heroic heart sweeps all aside, into the brilliant cadence of that final line. Oh, it's good!

If you can, find that peace within yourself, that peace and quiet and confidence that you can pass on to others, so that they know you are honest and you are fair and you will help them, no matter what, when the chips are down.

—MAJOR RICHARD D. "DICK" WINTERS, WORLD WAR II COMMANDER OF EASY COMPANY, 506TH REGIMENT, 101ST AIRBORNE DIVISION, IN *AMERICAN HISTORY* MAGAZINE, AUGUST 2004

On leadership, this is hard advice to quarrel with. Major Winters was a legendary leader of combat troops, made famous in Band of Brothers.

Don't flinch; don't foul; and hit the line hard.
—President Theodore Roosevelt, from his
commencement address to Georgetown
University's Class of 1906

Never flinch, never weary, never despair.
—Winston Churchill, from his last major speech
in the House of Commons

Good simple advice, well stated.

* * *

When duty calls, or danger, be never wanting there.
—Hymn: "Stand Up, Stand Up for Jesus"
by George Duffield

My father was fond of singing this line. Although he often sang it with a little twinkle of parody in his eye, it was a code he lived by. A little self-parody doesn't make something less true.

The tests of character come to us silently, unaware, by slow and inaudible approaches. We hardly know they are there, till lo! the hour has struck, and the choice has been made, well or ill, but whether well or ill, a choice. The heroic hours of life do not announce their presence by drum and trumpet, challenging us to be ourselves by appeals to the martial spirit that keeps the blood at heat. Some little, unassuming, unobtrusive choice presents itself before us slyly and craftily, glib and insinuating, in the modest garb of innocence. To yield to its blandishments is so easy. The wrong, it seems, is venial. Only hyper-sensitiveness, we assure ourselves, would call it wrong at all. These are the moments you will need to remember the game you are playing. Then it is you will be summoned to show the courage of adventurous youth.

—BENJAMIN CARDOZO

Choices between honor and dishonor are not announced with trumpets, and may have no audience but our own consciences. But there is no more important audience.

If I walk in the pathway of duty,

If I work 'til the close of the day

I shall see the great King in his beauty

When I walk the last mile of the way.

—HYMN: "THE LAST MILE OF THE WAY,"
JOHNSON OATMAN JR.

I have only sung this hymn in African American churches. I love its simple pacing and majestic confidence.

Far better it is to dare mighty things, to win glorious triumphs, even though checkered by failure, than to take rank with those poor spirits who neither enjoy much nor suffer much because they live in the gray twilight that knows neither victory nor defeat.

—THEODORE ROOSEVELT, APPOMATTOX DAY
SPEECH 1899

It is not the critic who counts; not the man who points out how the strong man stumbles, or where the doer of deeds could have done them better. The credit belongs to the man who is actually in the arena, whose face is marred by dust and sweat and blood; who strives valiantly; who errs and comes short again and again because there is no effort without error and shortcoming; but who does actually strive to do the deeds; who knows the great enthusiasms, the great devotions; who spends himself in a worthy cause; who at the best knows in the end the triumph of high achievement, and who at the worst, if he fails, at least fails while daring greatly, so that his place shall never be with those cold and timid souls who know neither victory nor defeat.

—THEODORE ROOSEVELT, "MAN IN THE ARENA"

These two statements by Teddy Roosevelt, the longer "Man in the Arena" speech and the shorter "gray twilight" version, are great expressions of the glory and merit of throwing yourself determinedly into something, and not holding back your effort in calculation of your chances, or standing aside entirely. A more laconic statement is Henry Kissinger's: "It is not possible to hedge against failure by half-hearted execution." Throw yourself in.

Hold on with a bulldog grip, and chew and choke as much as possible
  —ABRAHAM LINCOLN TO ULYSSES S. GRANT, 1864

Determination against an adversary has rarely been better or more graphically expressed. At last, President Lincoln had found a general willing to fight, and urged him on.

* * *

Aggressive fighting for the right is the noblest sport the world affords.
  —THEODORE ROOSEVELT

This is on a plaque in the Roosevelt Room at the White House. I copied it down at a meeting I attended there between President Clinton and his U.S. attorneys.

L evel of effort matters in most things in life.
   —ADVICE TO TOM AND MIKE DONILON FROM
   THEIR FATHER

Rhode Islanders Tom and Mike Donilon grew up in South Providence, and became, respectively, national security advisor to the president and counsel to the vice president.

I have in my own fashion learned the lesson that life is effort, unremittingly repeated, and . . . I feel somehow as if real pity were for those who had been beguiled into the perilous delusion that it isn't.
　　——HENRY JAMES

You must work very hard, because someone who is gifted has to work harder than someone who is not.
　　——MAURICE RAVEL

All I want is everything you've got for as long as it takes.
　　——DREW BLEDSOE

Work hard, not as a peon after pity or praise, but as a man strives determinedly to meet his duty to his kind.
　　——MARCUS AURELIUS

Work is the grand cure of all the maladies that ever test mankind.
—THOMAS CARLYLE

From a wide variety of backgrounds, a common message, echoing Virgil's at the beginning of the chapter. No way around it. Might as well enjoy it. And this is why:

The highest reward for man's toil is not what he gets for it, but what he becomes by it.
—JOHN RUSKIN

Thus,

Never despair; but if you do, work on in despair.
—EDMUND BURKE

Work nights and weekends. Most of your adversaries won't. You'll be amazed how much advantage you can get just by working nights and weekends when they're idle.

—GOVERNOR BRUCE SUNDLUN,
ENCOURAGING HIS STAFF

With Governor Sundlun, you could expect to be called at any hour. I learned an immense amount from him.

* * *

Whatever your work station, leave it better than you found it.

—ADVICE TO SENATOR JOHN CHAFEE FROM HIS FATHER

Senator Chafee occupied with great distinction the Senate seat I now hold. He was my father's lifelong friend, and an extraordinary servant of his state and country. This is as good advice as any.

[W]E SHALL NOT FLAG OR FAIL. We shall go on to the end, we shall fight in France, we shall fight on the seas and oceans, we shall fight with growing confidence and growing strength in the air, we shall defend our island, whatever the cost may be, we shall fight on the beaches, we shall fight on the landing grounds, we shall fight in the fields and in the streets, we shall fight in the hills; we shall never surrender.

—WINSTON CHURCHILL, "DUNKIRK" SPEECH

This is one of those quotes that everyone knows, that you can nearly recite, and that nevertheless is fresh and better every time you read it.

Wе fight, get beat, rise, and fight again.
—GENERAL NATHANAEL GREENE OF
RHODE ISLAND, TO HIS WIFE, 1781

General Greene was sent by George Washington to command the Revolutionary Army in the South. Despite never winning a battle, Greene's persistence kept sufficient British troops tied up in the South to allow the ultimate victory at Yorktown. Cornwallis's judgment: "Greene is more dangerous than Washington."

England expects every man to do his duty.
——ADMIRAL LORD NELSON

Before the Battle of Trafalgar, a victory, Lord Nelson sent this signal to his fleet from HMS Victory. *He was killed in that battle by a French sniper.*

* * *

Nobody made a greater mistake than he who did nothing because he could only do a little.
——EDMUND BURKE

And don't underestimate the consequences, in the right circumstances:

By gnawing through a dike, even a rat may drown a nation.
——EDMUND BURKE

Little strokes

Fell great oaks.

——BENJAMIN FRANKLIN, *POOR RICHARD'S ALMANAC*

So don't be discouraged.

A man walking along a beach covered in starfish that had been washed ashore saw a little girl throwing the starfish one by one back into the sea. "Don't bother," he said to the little girl, "There are far too many to save." The girl looked at a starfish, and threw it back in the sea. She looked up at the man. "I can save that one," she said.

This is one of the founding stories of City Year. I learned it the year I chaired the Rhode Island City Year board. It echoes Rabbi Tarfun's reminder I cite later that "it is not up to us to complete the work, but neither are we free to desist from it."

That which ordinary men are fit for, I am qualified in, and the best of me is diligence.

—THE DUKE OF KENT IN SHAKESPEARE'S
KING LEAR

Diligence is underrated. Thank you, Shakespeare.

Life is going to be difficult, and dreadful things will happen. What you do is to move along, get on with it, and be tough. Not in the sense of being mean to others, but tough with yourself and making a deadly effort not to be defeated.
—KATHARINE HEPBURN

Good tough advice from a good tough lady.

Keep Calm and Carry On.

Good steady advice for a good steady nation, from a poster produced by the British government as the Nazi threat loomed over their nation at the outset of World War II. Two and a half million were printed, but few were used. Evidently, the British people were sufficiently able to keep calm and carry on, without exhortation from the poster.

The heights by great men reached and kept

Were not attained by sudden flight,

But they, while their companions slept,

Were toiling upward in the night.

— HENRY WADSWORTH LONGFELLOW,
"THE LADDER OF ST. AUGUSTINE"

When my friend Patrick Kennedy left Congress, I used "toiling upward in the night" in my Senate speech to evoke how difficult his achievements had been for him. He persevered through immense challenges, very bravely, and to great effect.

A life of idle pleasure, even such pleasure as eighteenth-century Paris could provide, is incapable of satisfying the aspirations of a very intelligent man. And the reason of this is that work is a form of pleasure, and that man who has never worked has missed one of the great pleasures of life.

—DUFF COOPER, *TALLEYRAND*

Of all of life's luxuries, the ability to think of your work as a form of pleasure is among the greatest. In a strange personal aside about Duff Cooper, my father's cousin Susan Mary Alsop turned out to have had an affair with him in postwar Paris, and bore him a son, raised as her and her husband's child.

Work hard, then, on the disappointment or anti-climax which is certainly coming to the patient during his first weeks as a churchman. The Enemy allows this disappointment to occur on the threshold of every human endeavor. It occurs when the boy who has been enchanted in the nursery by *Stories from the Odyssey* buckles down to really learning Greek. It occurs when lovers have got married and begin the real task of learning to live together. In every department of life it marks the transition from dreamy aspiration to laborious doing.

—C. S. LEWIS

How often is this transition the time when resolution fails.

A stout heart breaks bad luck.
—SANCHO PANZA IN CERVANTES' DON QUIXOTE

* * *

When you go home, tell them of us and say,
"For your tomorrow, we gave our today."
—"KOHIMA EPITAPH," KOHIMA WAR MEMORIAL, INDIA

Go tell the Spartans, thou that passest by,
That here, faithful to their laws, we lie.
—"THERMOPYLAE EPITAPH," ATTRIBUTED TO SIMONIDES

There is no better expression of the price of duty than these two memorial epitaphs.

The badge of rank which an officer wears on his coat is really a symbol of servitude—servitude to his men.

—GENERAL MAXWELL D. TAYLOR, 1953

There is no better foundation for leadership than this sense of duty to one's team.

Spartans do not enquire how many the enemy are, only where they are.
—AGIS II, 427 B.C.

This fearless determination helps explain the deathless sacrifice at Thermopylae.

* * *

Determine that the thing can and shall be done, and then we shall find a way.
—ABRAHAM LINCOLN TO CONGRESS, 1848

Too often questions about how mask uncertainties about whether. This cuts straight through.

So nigh is grandeur to our dust,

So near is God to man,

When Duty whispers low, "Thou must,"

The youth replies, "I can."

—RALPH WALDO EMERSON, ON DUTY, IN
    "VOLUNTARIES"

This verse is inscribed on the war memorial in downtown Providence, RI. How nice that something as humble and available as duty connects dust to grandeur, man to God.

Don't condemn yourself or lose heart when you sometimes fail to measure up to your own principles; instead, get back up, embrace the imperfection of your own humanity, and go back with confidence and energy to your pursuit.
——MARCUS AURELIUS

I particularly like his advice not just to get back up and in it, but to do so with confidence and energy, even after a breakdown.

B eware of entrance to a quarrel: but being in, bear't that th' opposed may beware of thee.

——SHAKESPEARE, *HAMLET*

This is one of the precepts Polonius shares as advice to his son, Laertes, before Polonius is murdered by Hamlet.

Sundays too my father got up early
and put his clothes on in the blueblack cold,
then with cracked hands that ached
from labor in the weekday weather made
banked fires blaze. No one ever thanked him.
I'd wake and hear the cold splintering, breaking.
When the rooms were warm, he'd call,
and slowly I would rise and dress,
fearing the chronic angers of that house,
Speaking indifferently to him,
who had driven out the cold
and polished my good shoes as well.
What did I know, what did I know
of love's austere and lonely offices?
— ROBERT HAYDEN, "THOSE WINTER SUNDAYS"

"Blueblack cold" is a great phrase and image for winter morning, and the "austere and lonely offices" of love is a haunting expression. How easy it is to forget love's daily labors: "No one ever thanked him." Duty is an austere form of love, with none of its sentimental trappings.

CHAPTER THREE

HUMAN GOODNESS AND FOIBLE

Even leaky buckets carry water to the sick.

—HENRY D. SHARPE

Life is mostly froth and bubble;
Two things stand like stone:
Kindness in another's trouble,
Courage in one's own.
—ADAM LINDSAY GORDON IN "YE WEARIE WAYFARER"

I love this simple rhyme: jaunty and light; tactile and true.

To handle yourself, use your head.
To handle others, use your heart.
—ELEANOR ROOSEVELT

Another way of saying it, and an impeccable source.

No one cares how much you know, until they know how much you care.

Advice to Senator Joe Manchin from his grandmother, and very good advice.

About Philip II of Spain, the surpassing wooden-head of all sovereigns, "No experience of the failure of his policy could shake his belief in its essential excellence."
——BARBARA TUCHMAN, *MARCH OF FOLLY.*

Hmmm. What modern Americans might this bring to mind? And how many do we know like this in our own lives?

The threat to men of great dignity, privilege and pretense is not from the radicals they revile; it is from accepting their own myth. Exposure to reality remains the nemesis of the great—a little understood thing.
——JOHN KENNETH GALBRAITH IN *THE GREAT CRASH OF 1929* (1954)

I expect this is true of great people, or at least some. I am confident it is true of great institutions.

I cannot help expressing a wish that every member of the Convention who may still have objections to [the Constitution] would, with me, on this occasion, doubt a little of his own infallibility, and to make manifest our unanimity, put his name to this instrument.

—BENJAMIN FRANKLIN (1787)

Doubting a little of our own infallibility is doubt of the best kind. In the same vein, at the Constitutional Convention, James Madison wrote, "No man felt himself obliged to retain his opinions any longer than he was satisfied of their propriety and truth."

In matters that are obscure and far beyond our vision, even in such as we may find treated in Holy Scripture, different interpretations are sometimes possible without prejudice to the faith we have received. In such a case, we should not rush in headlong and so firmly take our stand on one side that, if further progress in the search for truth justly undermines this position, we too fall with it. That would be to battle not for the teaching of Holy Scripture, but for our own.

> —SAINT AUGUSTINE, *THE LITERAL MEANING OF GENESIS*,
> BOOK I, CHAPTER 18

Doubting certainty in religious matters can also be doubt of a good kind. I admire the caution and logic of Saint Augustine's embrace of flexibility in religious ideology, and I believe it helps lead to more humane results. And finally:

What is tolerance? It is the consequence of humanity. We are all formed of frailty and error; let us pardon reciprocally each other's folly—that is the first law of nature.

> —VOLTAIRE

This from a man who had very little reason to doubt his own infallibility.

I have a simple philosophy. Fill what's empty, empty what's full. Scratch where it itches.

—ALICE ROOSEVELT LONGWORTH

Sometimes the simplest things matter most.

* * *

Whenever Richard Cory went down town,
We people on the pavement looked at him:
He was a gentleman from sole to crown,
Clean favored and imperially slim.
And he was always quietly arrayed,
And he was always human when he talked;
But still he fluttered pulses when he said,
"Good Morning," and he glittered when he walked.
And he was rich—yes, richer than a king—
And admirably schooled in every grace:
In fine we thought that he was everything
To make us wish that we were in his place.
So on we worked, and waited for the light,
And went without the meat and cursed the bread;
And Richard Cory, one calm summer night,
Went home and put a bullet in his head.

—E. A. ROBINSON, "RICHARD CORY"

However good things may seem around you, or for others, this poem is a reminder that such appearances can be deceiving.

The reward for being honest is not that others will be honest in return—that is not my experience. The reward for being loving is not that others will be loving in return—that is not my experience. The reward for being honest is that it makes you an honest man, and the reward for being loving is that it makes you a loving man.

—EARL HIGHTOWER, MY BROTHER'S AA FRIEND

Earl is a friend of my brother Charlie, and guided him through rehabilitation from drug and alcohol addiction. He said this as the invited speaker at a meeting I attended with Charlie, and I have never forgotten it. I am indebted to him for my brother's wonderful life.

A Scout is trustworthy, loyal, helpful, friendly, courteous, kind, obedient, cheerful, thrifty, brave, clean, and reverent.

—BOY SCOUT LAW

These values are always worth remembering. Even eight out of twelve is an achievement. We all know people who don't get to six on their best day!

We more normally act our way into a manner of thinking than think our way into a manner of acting.
—WILLIAM C. SPOHN

We do not see things as they are. We see things as we are.

I don't know the source for the second saying. These are well worth keeping in mind in evaluating our own opinions.

It ain't what you don't know that gets you in trouble, it's what you know for sure that just ain't so.

—MARK TWAIN

Ain't that the truth?

It's difficult to get a man to understand something when his salary depends upon his not understanding it.
—UPTON SINCLAIR

A simple truism from Al Gore's An Inconvenient Truth: *Hire a lobbyist and it gets worse! Make it a corporation or an industry instead of a man, and it becomes hopeless. Psychologists call it "motivated reasoning"—the more motivated, the less reasoning!*

T alleyrand: "the greatest modern statesman, because he had so well known when it was necessary both to suffer wrong to be done and to do it."

—ALEXANDER HAMILTON

A tough-minded American talking about a tough-minded Frenchman. Diplomacy can be a quietly brutal game.

When some of these sons of bitches start thinking, they weaken the team.

——GENERAL FREDERICK "BRICK" KRAUSE, VIETNAM,
AS REPORTED BY MY FATHER

General Krause was a close and admired friend of my father's, from their Vietnam war years together. This became one of my father's favorite phrases. It was not uncommon for one of his children to be found "weakening the team." Anybody who has managed others any length of time understands this observation. But have you ever heard it better stated?

A proud warrior approached an old monk and asked him to describe heaven and hell. The old monk replied, "You filthy lout, I would never speak to one so vile as you." Enraged, the warrior drew his sword to kill the monk. "That," the monk said, "is hell." Seeing the monk's teaching, the warrior sheathed his sword and bowed. "And that, my son, is heaven," said the monk.
——UNKNOWN, AND LIKELY APOCRYPHAL

A good story and a good lesson.

Anyone can become angry—that is easy. But to be angry with the right person, to the right degree, at the right time, for the right purpose, and in the right way—this is not easy.
——ARISTOTLE, *THE NICOMACHEAN ETHICS*

Similarly, a good reminder about anger's role.

One ought not to be obstinate, except when one ought to be; but when one ought to be, then one ought to be unshakable.
——CHARLES-MAURICE DE TALLEYRAND-PÉRIGORD,
QUOTED IN DUFF COOPER'S *TALLEYRAND*

And a similar reminder about obstinacy.

to hell with anything unrefined has always been my motto

. . . .

o wotthehell o toujours gai i never had time to fret

i danced to whatever tune was played and there s life in the

old dame yet

—THE CAT MEHITABEL, AS REPORTED BY THE
COCKROACH ARCHY, FROM *ARCHY AND MEHITABEL*

You probably won't understand this if you haven't read Don Marquis's archy and mehitabel. *Eighty years later, it still rocks the house. You are in for a treat.*

Speak not evil of the absent, for it is unjust.

Another (no. 89) of George Washington's 110 "Rules of Civility." This one is very hard to honor. I wonder if Washington always did.

* * *

Persuasion, perseverance and patience are the best advocates on questions depending on the will of others.
—THOMAS JEFFERSON

These words are good to remember when working with others.

The versatility of circumstances often mocks a natural desire for definitiveness.

—WIENER V. UNITED STATES, 357 U.S. 349, 352 (1958)

Yes, and we are often tangled up in the mess that results. A good alert against the doctrinaire.

It is [the poet's and writer's] privilege to help man endure by lifting up his heart, by reminding him of the courage and honor and hope and pride and compassion and pity and sacrifice which have been the glory of his past.
—WILLIAM FAULKNER, NOBEL PRIZE SPEECH, 1950

A messy, but moving, sentence.

✳ ✳ ✳

When something outside of yourself pains and disturbs you, remember that it is not the thing itself, but your judgments about it, that cause you pain and disturbance. These judgments being yours, they are in your power to erase.
—MARCUS AURELIUS

I know a man who lost his wife to illness, his child to accident, and his home to fire. Against loses of this magnitude, this advice seems trite; against the day-to-day annoyances life presents it is a worthy reminder of who's in charge of our attitude, mood, and morale. Maintaining good morale in bad circumstances is a special and underrated form of courage. Auschwitz survivor Viktor Frankl saw the best and worst of what mankind is capable of, and wrote, "everything can be taken away from a man but one thing: the last of human freedoms—to choose one's own attitude in any given circumstances, to choose one's own way."

W e are apt to shut our eyes against a painful truth, and listen to the song of that siren till she transforms us into beasts.

—PATRICK HENRY, "LIBERTY OR DEATH" SPEECH

The siren was hope. As the world gets more complex, and the painful truths get more dangerous, it is wise to remember this.

And on the pedestal these words appear:
"My name is Ozymandias, King of Kings:
Look upon my Works, ye Mighty, and despair!"
Nothing beside remains. Round the decay
Of that colossal Wreck, boundless and bare
The lone and level sands stretch far away.
—Percy Bysshe Shelley, "Ozymandias of Egypt"

The inevitability of loss; the vanity of pride; the stark image of failure—unforgettable.

Even in our sleep,

pain which cannot forget

falls drop by drop upon the heart

until, in our own despair, against our will,

comes wisdom through the awful grace of God.

—AESCHYLUS, FROM *AGAMEMNON*, AS QUOTED BY
ROBERT F. KENNEDY AFTER LEARNING THAT
MARTIN LUTHER KING JR. WAS SHOT

This wrenchingly beautiful piece of poetry and human observation, is made more wrenching by the image of Robert F. Kennedy reciting it to a black audience, delivering the news of Martin Luther King Jr.'s assassination, two months and a day before his own. It appears to be a slight misquotation of the Edith Hamilton translation: "And even in our sleep, pain that cannot forget falls drop by drop upon the heart, and in our own despite against our will, comes wisdom to us by the awful grace of God." Under the stress of that moment and its awful news, he had the presence of mind to recite it so accurately.

CHAPTER FOUR

ARGUMENT AND ANALOGY

I love argument. I love debate. I didn't
expect anyone just to sit there and agree with me.
That's not their job.

—MARGARET THATCHER

[HITLER] MUST BLOOD HIS HOUNDS and show them sport, or else, like Actaeon of old, be devoured by them.

> —WINSTON CHURCHILL'S SPEECH TO THE PEOPLE OF THE UNITED STATES, "THE DEFENSE OF FREEDOM AND PEACE," OCTOBER 16, 1938 (ACTAEON'S HOUNDS SLEW HIM WHEN HE WAS TURNED INTO A STAG UPON SEEING DIANA BATHING)

Compare Actaeon's fate to that of Diomedes:

Who was devoured by those horses whom he had himself taught to feed on the flesh and blood of men.

— THOMAS BABINGTON MACAULAY

Jefferson captures that animal power:

We have the wolf by the ears, and we can neither hold him nor safely let him go.

Compare that to John F. Kennedy's inaugural address:

Those who foolishly sought power by riding the back of the tiger ended up inside.

This is perhaps a reference to Churchill, in 1937:

Dictators ride to and fro upon tigers from which they dare not dismount. And the tigers are getting hungry.

President Kennedy's father was appointed Ambassador to the Court of St. James shortly after that speech and so the young JFK was likely aware of it as he wrote Why England Slept. *These are all good stories and analogies for animal forces that, once set in motion, become uncontrollable and dangerous, and become the master of the man.*

One of those plain propositions which reasoning cannot render plainer.
—CHIEF JUSTICE JOHN MARSHALL IN *WAYMAN V. SOUTHARD,* 23 U.S. 1, 22, 10 WHEAT 1, 43 (1825)

This is one of those truths, which to a correct and unprejudiced mind, carries its own evidence along with it; and may be obscured, but cannot be made plainer by argument or reasoning.
—ALEXANDER HAMILTON, *THE FEDERALIST* NO. 23

These are axioms so self-evident that no explanation can make them plainer.
—THOMAS JEFFERSON 1823 (LETTER TO THOMAS EARLE)

This is so obviously the necessary result of the Constitution that it has rarely been called into question and hence authorities directly dealing with it do not abound.

> —*New York Life Ins. Co. v. Head*, 234 U.S. 149, 161 (1914)

. . . too plain to require further discussion.

> —*United States v. Nixon*, 418 U.S. 683, 705 (1974)

A lawyer sometimes finds the proposition he is searching for through case law to be so self-evident that it has never been stated. Yet judges expect legal authority supporting a proposition, and it is the lawyer's duty to provide it. These useful citations, to exemplary authorities (Marshall, Hamilton, and Jefferson), meet that circumstance; a valuable tool in the legal advocate's toolbox.

These are the times that try men's souls. The summer soldier and the sunshine patriot will, in this crisis, shrink from the service of their country.

—THOMAS PAINE, *THE AMERICAN CRISIS*

The "summer soldier and the sunshine patriot" are the original fair-weather friend. The power of this image is echoed by Clarence Darrow, in this 1895 speech:

The ordinary fair-weather patriot goes out upon the street corners, and in public places, and proclaims his love for American institutions as a cloak for the support for existing wrongs, which make him rich and great; he uses his patriotism as he does the other tools with which he plies his trade; patriotism to him does not mean devotion to his country and the people's highest good, but a blind, unthinking worship of things as they are; the constitution and laws, to him, are to be either enforced or broken as it may profit at the time; his is a patriotism that flies an American flag from the schoolhouse, and sacrifices the most vital and fundamental principles of liberty for gain.

—CLARENCE DARROW, CHICAGO, NOVEMBER 1895

Nicodemus—the Pharisee and ruler of the Jews who came to see Jesus, but only in the dark of night.

—JOHN 3:1–2

A great example of a faint or cautious heart: a man who fears his own convictions.

A n argument not made has some weight, as it shows that the argument "neither occurred to the bar or the bench."

> —*UNITED STATES v. ROSS*, 456 U.S. 798, 819 (1982), QUOTING *BANK OF THE UNITED STATES v. DEVEAUX*, 5 U.S. (CRANCH) 61, 88 (1791).

This happens sometimes, and this citation allows the advocate to address it.

And they shall beat their swords into plowshares,

and their spears into pruning hooks;

Nation shall not lift up sword against nation,

neither shall they learn war anymore.

—Isaiah 2:4

Beat your plowshares into swords

And your pruning hooks into spears;

—Joel 3:10

I have always wondered about this. I think of it when someone relies too hard on a particular authority, and am reminded that even the Bible can offer contrary messages.

St. Anthony the Hermit, who refused to do right when the devil told him to.

—CITED BY WINSTON CHURCHILL IN HIS 1938 SPEECH, "THE AIR DEFENSES OF BRITAIN"

A great example of mistaking the agent for the principle.

*   *   *

The perfect is the enemy of the good.

—ATTRIBUTED TO VOLTAIRE AND DEMOSTHENES

I do not want the best to be any more the deadly enemy of the good.

—BISHOP DOANE, QUOTED IN *THE STRENUOUS LIFE*, THEODORE ROOSEVELT

This oft-quoted observation has many attributions. The only place I've actually run across it quoted was in Teddy Roosevelt's The Strenuous Life. *A wise thing, particularly in negotiations, not to let the perfect be the enemy of the good.*

We have always known that heedless self-interest was bad morals; now we know that is bad economics.
—FRANKLIN D. ROOSEVELT, 1937

A spare and elegant statement of a good point.

Americans . . . are fond of explaining almost all the actions of their lives by the principle of self-interest rightly understood; they show with complacency how an enlightened regard for themselves constantly prompts them to assist one another and inclines them willingly to sacrifice a portion of their time and property to the welfare of the state.
—ALEXIS DE TOCQUEVILLE, *DEMOCRACY IN AMERICA*

I refute it thus!

—SAMUEL JOHNSON, TO HIS BIOGRAPHER JAMES BOSWELL, KICKING A LARGE STONE OUT OF THE ROAD, AFTER BEING ASKED HOW HE WOULD REFUTE THE SPEECH OF BISHOP BERKELEY THEY HAD JUST HEARD, SUGGESTING THE NONEXISTENCE OF MATTER.

This is a good reminder that a complex argument does not require a complex counterargument. A related story tells of my predecessor in the Senate, John O. Pastore. Responding to a lengthy peroration against the measure he was proposing, he declared in his booming voice, "So what!" and asked for the yeas and nays.

"Let them stand undisturbed as monuments of the safety with which error of opinion may be tolerated where reason is left free to combat it."

—THOMAS JEFFERSON, FROM HIS INAUGURAL ADDRESS.

In his Inaugural Address, President Jefferson takes on those "who would wish to dissolve this Union or to change its Republican form." A nice combination of backhanded compliment to our Republic's strength, and devastating criticism of those holding such views.

* * *

There are two kinds of light: the glow that illumines, and the glare that obscures.

—JAMES THURBER, *LANTERNS AND LANCES*

The transition from "light" to "glare" to "obscure" is well done, and of course the point is true.

Stubbornness and stupidity are twins.

—SOPHOCLES, *ANTIGONE*

This quotation provides a polite way to couch a harsh point.

Statistics are a pleasant indoor sport—not so good as crossword puzzles—and they prove nothing to any sensible person who is familiar with statistics.

There is nothing that lies like statistics.

   —CLARENCE DARROW, 1924

Always handy when presented with statistics.

We are not enemies, but friends. We must not be enemies. Though passion may have strained it must not break our bonds of affection. The mystic chords of memory, stretching from every battlefield and patriot grave to every living heart and hearthstone all over this broad land, will yet swell the chorus of the Union, when again touched, as surely they will be, by the better angels of our nature.

—ABRAHAM LINCOLN

In seeking a decent propriety from the other side in a dispute, appealing to the "better angels of their nature" has this historic precedent. To see Lincoln's talent with words, consider the original proposal from Secretary of State William Seward:

I close. We are not, we must not be, aliens or enemies, but fellow countrymen and brethren. Although passion has strained our bonds of affection too hardly, they must not, I am sure they will not, be broken. The mystic chords which, proceeding from so many battle-fields and patriot graves, pass through all the hearts and all the hearths in this broad continent of ours, will yet again harmonize in their ancient music when breathed upon by the guardian angels of the nation.

Seward supplied the building blocks; Lincoln made the magic.

A very wholesome and comfortable doctrine, to which we can have but one objection, namely, that it is not true.

> —HENRY FIELDING, *THE HISTORY OF TOM JONES* BOOK XV CHAPTER 1 (SPEAKING OF THE NOTION THAT VIRTUE IS REWARDED). SEE *IN RE GLOBE NEWSPAPER CO.*, 729 F. 2D 47, AT 54 (1ST CIRCUIT COURT OF APPEALS, 1984)

Comfortable doctrines often suffer this flaw. I like the way this is said.

* * *

Frequently an issue of this sort will come before the Court clad, so to speak, in sheep's clothing. . . .But this wolf comes as a wolf.

> —*MORRISON V. OLSON*, 487 U.S. 654, 699, 1988 (JUSTICE ANTONIN SCALIA, DISSENTING).

A great phrase by a sometimes infuriating but brilliant and phrase-worthy judge. I have used this often.

To prevent slipping, a knot depends on friction, and to provide friction, there must be pressure of some sort. This pressure and the place within the knot where it occurs is called the nip. The security of a knot seems to depend solely on its nip.

——*THE ASHLEY BOOK OF KNOTS*

The simple mechanics of this, and its discussion of an everyday device so simple its operation is usually overlooked, and the resulting phrase "the nip of the knot," all appeal to me.

[T]HE STAIRWAY . . . leads to a dark gulf. It is a fine, broad stairway at the beginning, but after a bit the carpet ends. A little farther on there are only flagstones, and a little farther on still these break beneath your feet.

—WINSTON CHURCHILL, SPEECH IN COMMONS, MARCH 24, 1938

The image of the dark stairway and the stones ultimately crumbling beneath your feet is compelling. I used it to argue against the Bush administration's tolerance of torture.

The flies that keep the oxen from ploughing.
— CHEKHOV ON REVIEWERS AND CRITICS

For when the kibitzers and critics are bothering you, and distracting you from your work. They are turning no earth; they are creating no furrow; they are readying no planting. They merit your sympathy as much as your ire.

* * *

You have sat too long here for any good you have been doing. Depart, I say, and let us have done with you. In the name of God, go!
— LORD CROMWELL, TO THE LONG PARLIAMENT

For when it is necessary to send someone unceremoniously on their way. The most momentous modern use of this quotation was on May 7, 1940, by a young member of Parliament. As war loomed over England, and the Chamberlain government dithered, Leo Amery took the floor of the House of Commons to condemn the aging prime minister, of his own party, across the well of the House. He ended with this quote. Harold Macmillan, years later to become prime minister himself, was present and described it as "the most formidable philippic which I have ever heard." The Chamberlain government shortly thereafter collapsed.

Facts are stubborn things; and whatever may be our wishes, our inclinations, or the dictates of passion, they cannot alter the state of the facts and the evidence.

—JOHN ADAMS, FROM HIS CLOSING ARGUMENT TO THE JURY, DEFENDING BRITISH SOLDIERS WHO FIRED IN THE BOSTON MASSACRE

Similar is the famous observation of New York Senator Daniel Patrick Moynihan: "You are entitled to your own opinion. You are not entitled to your own facts." Related is the parliamentary riposte, attributed to Richard Brinsley Sheridan, "The Right Honorable gentleman is indebted to his memory for his jests, and to his imagination for his facts." Constantly grounding your argument in the facts is a tactic of good advocacy, as is, as Adams did, countering passion, suspicion, and predisposition with stubborn facts.

CHAPTER FIVE

WORDS AND PHRASES

When you come to think of it, there is nothing in the world so powerful—and so powerless—as a word.

—IVAN TURGENEV, *TORRENTS OF SPRING*

False words are not only evil in themselves, but they infect the soul with evil.

—SOCRATES, PLATO'S *DEATH OF SOCRATES*

* * *

Strunk and White's *Elements of Style*, as summarized by Zechariah Chafee:

1. Write with definite, specific, concise language.
2. Write with nouns and verbs.
3. Omit needless words.
4. Be clear.
5. Use the active voice.
6. Put yourself in the background.
7. Make the paragraph the unit of composition.
8. Pick a design and stick to it.
9. Put statements in the positive form.
10. Avoid the elaborate, pretentious, coy, or cute.

My friend Zechariah Chafee is an excellent writer, indeed the best speechwriter I know. His eulogy for his father was the best speech I've ever heard any friend deliver. Here he summarizes Strunk and White.

And rotten from the gunwale to the keel,

Rat-riddled, bilge-bestank,

Slime-slobbered, horrible, I saw her reel,

And drag her oozy flank,

And sprawl among the deft young waves, that laughed,

And leapt, and turned in many a sportive wheel,

As she thumped onward with her lumbering draught.

—A STANZA FROM THOMAS EDWARD BROWN'S
"THE SCHOONER"

Avoid all clichés like the plague.
　　—WILLIAM SAFIRE

Get it?

* * *

Covin—a collusive agreement between persons to prejudice another.

Gambado—a little decorative leap made by a horse in which all four feet leave the ground but the horse goes nowhere.

Pelf—riches or wealth, especially when fraudulently obtained.

Purfle—to decorate the edge or border (noun and verb).

Terrets—the loops in a harness through which the reins go.

Widdershins, also withershins—backwards, contrarily, opposite to the natural direction.

All great, odd words: "terrets," "purfle," and "gambado" particularly lend themselves to analogy.

They work every day. . . . They catch the early bus.

—REVEREND JESSE JACKSON

In his concession speech at the Democratic Convention, Reverend Jackson pushed back against the suggestion that the poor are lazy, using this memorable image.

In the bleak midwinter

Frosty wind made moan,

Earth stood hard as iron,

Water like a stone;

Snow had fallen, snow on snow,

Snow on snow,

In the bleak midwinter,

Long ago.

—Christina Rossetti, "In the Bleak Midwinter"

Nice work on winter with small words.

Honest plain words best pierce the ear of grief.
—SHAKESPEARE, *LOVE'S LABOURS LOST,* ACT 5, SCENE 2

Small words are the best ones, and old small words are the best of all.
—WINSTON CHURCHILL

Two of the English language's greatest masters, agreeing on this basic point. This is a really good point. It is virtually never wrong. Keep it simple.

Use it up; wear it out;

Make it do, or do without.

—BELTON A. COPP IV

A phrase of a dear friend's father, nicely matching the frugality of words with the frugality it describes.

The essence of dramatic tragedy is not unhappiness. It resides in the solemnity of the remorseless working of things.
—ALFRED NORTH WHITEHEAD

A radical is a person with both feet firmly planted in the air.
—FRANKLIN D. ROOSEVELT

Markets overshoot.
—ROGER ALTMAN, AT A DEMOCRATIC POLICY
COMMITTEE LUNCH IN THE SENATE

The Bush administration is "impervious to information."
—SENATOR JOSEPH BIDEN, IRAQ DEBATE

A judiciary independent of the nation and which from the citadel of the law, can turn its guns on those they were meant to defend. . . .
—PRESIDENT THOMAS JEFFERSON,
ON THE AARON BURR TRIAL

All good and useful phrases in argument or discussion. I particularly like "the solemnity of the remorseless working of things," and the citadel "turn[ing] its guns on those they were meant to defend." But on to the champion:

It is a riddle wrapped in a mystery inside an enigma.
>—WINSTON CHURCHILL, *THE GATHERING STORM*,
>ON RUSSIA

Like an inebriate regulating a chronometer with a crowbar.
>—WINSTON CHURCHILL, ON WILLIAM JENNINGS BRYAN

A dark hand, at first gloved in folly, now intervenes.
>—WINSTON CHURCHILL, ON THE ASSASSINATION OF
>CZAR NICHOLAS II

The morning had been golden; the noontide was bronze; and the evening lead.
>—WINSTON CHURCHILL, ON THE DECLINING STATURE
>OF LORD CURZON, VICEROY OF INDIA. HE ADDED:
>"BUT ALL WERE SOLID, AND EACH WAS POLISHED 'TIL
>IT SHONE AFTER ITS FASHION."

The tiny things, the sharp agate points, on which the ponderous balance of destiny turns.
>—WINSTON CHURCHILL, "IF LEE HAD NOT WON THE
>BATTLE OF GETTYSBURG"

The master of phrases. All also good and useful in argument or discussion. I frequently use "the sharp agate points." And how often does history's dark hand first come "gloved in folly."

Who is in charge of the clattering train?

The axles creak and the couplings strain;

and the pace is hot and the points are near,

and Sleep has deadened the driver's ear;

and the signals flash through the night in vain,

For Death is in charge of the clattering train.

—A STANZA FROM EDWIN JAMES MILLIKEN'S
"DEATH AND HIS BROTHER SLEEP"

Winston Churchill quoted this poem in his 1948 book The Gathering Storm *on the events leading up World War II, expressing the distress of those who saw England hurtling unprepared toward war. The currency of this image prewar is suggested by the famous CBS correspondent Edward R. Murrow telling his American radio audience that the sentiment of the British people was that "the machinery is out of control, that we are all passengers on an express train traveling at high speed through a dark tunnel toward an unknown destiny. We sit and talk as convincingly as we can, speaking words someone else has used. The suspicion recurs that the train may have no engineer, no one who can handle it."*

S uffer no man and no cause to escape the undying penalty which history has the power to inflict on wrong.

—LORD ACTON'S ADVICE TO HISTORIANS

The "undying penalty which history has the power to inflict on wrong" is often the last hope of those gone down to defeat against that wrong. In the Senate, I dread the undying penalty which history will inflict on our folly and ignorance in failing to address our carbon pollution and the changes it is wreaking on our world. This phrase haunts me.

Come on, Sheldon, strap on your ass-kissing lips— we're going up to the legislature.

—CHIEF JUSTICE RICHARD F. NEELY, WEST VIRGINIA SUPREME COURT, 1983

I was sitting in my office, scrivening away as a law clerk to Justice Neely, who had responsibility that year for getting the court's budget through the West Virginia legislature. As part of my education, he invited me to tag along, with this memorable phrase.

The moon was a ghostly galleon, tossed upon cloudy seas . . .
— ALFRED NOYES, "THE HIGHWAYMAN"

You may hear that Edward is cold and calculating. This is not the
case. Edward is warm and calculating.
— PROFESSOR PHIL KURLAND, OF ATTORNEY GENERAL
EDWARD LEVI

A full seven-horse-tail pasha.
— SEE BASHA (N.) IN FOWLER'S MODERN ENGLISH
USAGE, 3RD EDITION

He loves me like a glutton loves his lunch.
— KATHARINE HEPBURN AS ELEANOR OF AQUITAINE
IN *THE LION IN WINTER*

These phrases are just fun or telling.

CHAPTER SIX

LAW, LIBERTY, AND POLITICS

How small, of all that human hearts endure,
that part which kings or laws can cause or cure.

—SAMUEL JOHNSON

One thing I supplicate, your majesty: that you will give orders, under a great penalty, that no bachelors of law should be allowed to come to her (the New World); for not only are they bad themselves, but they also make and contrive a thousand iniquities.

——VASCO NÚÑEZ DE BALBOA TO KING FERDINAND V OF SPAIN, 1513

Well, we've seen how that worked out.

J ustice removed, then, what are kingdoms but great
bands of robbers?

—SAINT AUGUSTINE

The Democratic senators held a day-long caucus after the inauguration of President Obama. During our discussion, Robert Casey, the senator from Pennsylvania, quoted this phrase. I wrote it down in my meeting notes and copied it into my book.

Democracy is no easy form of government. Few nations have been able to sustain it. For it requires that we take the chances of freedom; that the liberating play of reason be brought to bear on events filled with passion; that dissent be allowed to make an appeal for acceptance; that men chance error in their search for truth.

I have found this quote attributed both to President Kennedy and to his brother Robert. For both men, extensive reading in history made the political process come alive in ways few other politicians have understood, and they each brought to it a sense of daring we do well to remember.

The real importance of the Inquisition is not so much in the awful solemnities of the auto-da-fé, nor in the cases of a few celebrated victims, but in the silent influence exercised by its incessant and secret labors among the mass of the people and the limitations which it placed on the Spanish intellect.

—HENRY CHARLES LEA, ON THE INQUISITION, FROM *INQUISITION: THE REIGN OF FEAR*, BY TOBY GREEN

This observation reflects the value of an unhindered search for truth in the development of societies. The degradation of the Spanish Empire's intellectual and economic development was the ultimate price of the Inquisition's oppressive orthodoxy, setting aside its brutality. Ideological fixity has a real price.

Politics, it is truly said, is the "art of the possible." But great causes only prevail through the vigor and energy of resolute men who attempt—and succeed—in making the impossible possible.

—PAUL EMRYS-EVANS, MEMBER OF PARLIAMENT, 1931–1945, FROM TROUBLESOME YOUNG MEN

Related is Margaret Mead's observation: "Never doubt that a small group of thoughtful, committed citizens can change the world. Indeed, it is the only thing that ever has."

One of the chief virtues of a democracy, however, is that its defects are always visible, and under democratic processes can be pointed out and corrected.

—HARRY S. TRUMAN

Democracy's virtue is not that it is free of defects.

My experience in government is that when things are non-controversial, beautifully coordinated and all the rest, it must be that there is not much going on.

—PRESIDENT JOHN F. KENNEDY

The seeming chaos of drawing out disagreement in Congress is an efficient process. It's when it does not happen that Congress becomes inefficient. Disagreement . . . the clear defining of disagreement, and the eventual resolving of disagreement is what makes for good legislation, and therefore is efficient.

—EDMUND MUSKIE, IN BERNARD ASBELL'S *THE SENATE NOBODY KNOWS,* P. 211

If efficiency means swift action, then it should not be a primary objective for Congress. It is a mistake to equate efficiency with effectiveness. . . . I sense sometimes that Congress is operating most effectively when it appears to be functioning in total chaos.

—*THE SENATE NOBODY KNOWS,* QUOTING CHARLES FERRIS, MUSKIE STAFF, P. 211

These observations are from veterans of legislative and executive politics. When everything is beautifully coordinated and appears efficient, it could mean that a show is being put on for you, and you have missed the real deal. Muskie's thought is very sophisticated, but very real, and very human. It understands why we legislate, when we are doing it right. Legislation can be a mere clash of wills, but at its heart it is a structure for drawing out the elements of, and bringing to an orderly conclusion, lively, even bitter, national conversations and debates.

Treason . . . is the charge which is most capable of being employed as the instrument of those malignant and vindictive passions which may rage in the bosoms of contending parties struggling for power.

—JOHN MARSHALL, IN THE AARON BURR TRIAL

Malignant and vindictive passions indeed do rage sometimes, and Marshall describes it with vigor. I have used this.

Making sport of Congress has a long tradition. Speaker Nicholas Longworth, an Ohio Republican, said in 1925 that he had been a member of Congress for twenty years, but "during the whole of that time we have been attacked, denounced, despised, hunted, harried, blamed, looked down upon, excoriated, and flayed. I refuse to take it personally . . . we have always been unpopular. From the beginning of the Republic, it has been the duty of every free-born voter to look down upon us and the duty of every free-born humorist to make jokes at us."

—ELIZABETH DREW, "ENOUGH WITH THE
MISLEADING WORDS ABOUT CONGRESS,"
POLITICO SEPTEMBER 9, 2010

Elizabeth Drew has, over many decades, done some of the best writing about American politics and government. She used this wonderful, good-hearted quotation acknowledging the cheerful disrespect Americans have for their elected officials.

Many forms of government have been tried and will be tried, in this world of sin and woe. No one pretends that democracy is perfect or all-wise. Indeed it has been said that democracy is the worst form of government except for all those other forms that have been tried from time to time

—WINSTON CHURCHILL

When democracy tries our patience, this is good to remember.

Political language . . . is designed to make lies sound truthful and murder respectable, and to give an appearance of solidity to pure wind.

—George Orwell, "Politics and the English Language"

True of at least some political language; another vigorous description!

Magnanimity in politics is not seldom the truest wisdom.
—EDMUND BURKE

This statement is inscribed on the base of the statue of Edmund Burke that stands on Massachusetts Avenue near 11th Street in Washington, D.C. The full quotation as delivered by Burke concludes: "and a great empire and little minds go ill together."

Whatever one may think about democratic government, it is just as well to have practical experience of its rough and slatternly foundations.

—WINSTON CHURCHILL, *MAXIMS AND REFLECTIONS*

Winston Churchill loved politics and the occasion politics provides to intermingle ideas, humanity (warts and all), aspirations, goals, interests, and emotions. Democratic government can be messy, but its feet of clay make its noblest demonstrations all the more inspiring.

The Greek republics of antiquity sometimes placed some particular law under a special sanction by denouncing the penalty of death to anyone who should propose to repeal it. In such cases, the man who intended to repeal the law so sanctioned of course began by proposing the repeal of the law which imposed the penalty.

— JAMES BRYCE, THE AMERICAN COMMONWEALTH, VOL. 1

There is always a way around in politics. This is a nice simple illustration. When I enter the Senate side of the Capitol, just beyond the elevators in an alcove on the right is a beautiful bust of Bryce, describing him as a "Friend and Ambassador to the American People and Interpreter of their Institutions."

Procedure is the bone structure of a democratic society; and the quality of procedural standards which meet general acceptance—the quality of what is tolerable and permissible and acceptable conduct—determines the durability of the society and the survival possibilities of freedom within the society.

—ABE FORTAS, *CONCERNING DISSENT AND CIVIL DISOBEDIENCE (1968)*

Our democracy concerns itself with rights and restrictions, benefits and penalties, but beneath it all, and making that discussion possible in an orderly and ultimately conclusive way, is the bone structure of legislative, judicial, and administrative procedure.

D

on't underestimate listening. Do not underestimate listening.

——KENNETH FEINBERG

From a man who did a lot of listening to people who had done a lot of suffering. Ken Feinberg administered for the government the compensation funds for the victims of the September 11 attack and the British Petroleum explosion and oil spill in the Gulf of Mexico.

In most matters it is more important that the applicable rule of law be settled than that it be settled right.
—JUSTICE LOUIS D. BRANDEIS, DISSENTING IN *BURNETT V. CORONADO OIL & GAS CO.*, 285 U.S. 393 (1932)

This is true surprisingly frequently. Clarity is a high virtue, apart from the substance. Jefferson in his Manual of Parliamentary Practice *made the same point: "It is much more material that there should be a rule to go by, than what the rule is."*

Touch base with those concerned before taking action.

—GOVERNOR SUNDLUN

In politics, it is ordinarily better that people are informed of actions, particularly of actions or decisions against their interests. Failing to inform turns a small injury into a large one, and a large injury into a catastrophic one. Governor Sundlun had signs made for the desks of all his senior staff as a reminder of this practical political fact.

I was outvoted, having only reason on my side.
—SOUTH CAROLINA LEGISLATOR JOHN LAURENS,
WRITING TO ALEXANDER HAMILTON

Putting the best face on a solitary defeat.

* * *

Necessity impels me to speak true rather than pleasant things.
—FROM DANIEL WEBSTER'S DEDICATION ON THE
PRINTED COPIES OF HIS "SEVENTH OF MARCH" 1850
SPEECH, REPORTED IN *PROFILES IN COURAGE*

The great balance of democracy is the balance between telling people what they want to hear, and telling people what they need to know. The former is irresponsible; the latter can be suicidal. But when necessity counsels, duty is clear.

I went to bed at about 3 A.M. I was conscious of a profound sense of relief. At last I had authority to give directions over the whole scene. I felt as if I were walking with Destiny, and that all my past life had been but a preparation for this hour and for this trial. Eleven years in the political wilderness had freed me from ordinary party antagonisms. My warnings over the last six years had been so numerous, so detailed, and were now so terribly vindicated, that no one could gainsay me. I could not be reproached either for making the war or with want of preparation for it. I thought I knew a good deal about it all, and I was sure I should not fail. Therefore, although impatient for the morning, I slept soundly and had no need for cheering dreams. Facts are better than dreams.

— WINSTON CHURCHILL, THE GATHERING STORM

Winston Churchill describes his election as prime minister at the beginning of World War II with a remarkable sense of calm, confidence, and alignment with history's current. In the shadow of the looming Nazi peril, it is an extraordinary attribute of character. An emblem of his determined leadership is the direction "ACTION THIS DAY" stamped on orders he deemed urgent.

I never gave anybody hell. I just told the truth and they thought it was hell.

—"GIVE 'EM HELL" HARRY S. TRUMAN

Nicely done, Mr. President.

Hostility against every tyranny over the mind of man.

—THOMAS JEFFERSON, JEFFERSON MEMORIAL

This phrase is carved in the Jefferson memorial.

I know there is a God and I know He hates injustice. I see the storm coming and I know His hand is in it. But if he has a place and a part for me, I believe that I am ready.
—ABRAHAM LINCOLN, 1860, WRITING TO A FRIEND DURING HIS CAMPAIGN FOR THE PRESIDENCY

This quote, attributed to Abraham Lincoln in the shadow of the country's slip toward Civil War, was used by then-Senator John F. Kennedy 100 years later while speaking to the crowd gathered at his last campaign stop, in Providence, in what would thereafter be called Kennedy Plaza. I attended the fiftieth anniversary of that speech with his nephew, Congressman Patrick Kennedy. In a noteworthy contrast, Thomas Jefferson in his Inaugural Address declared his "sincere consciousness that the task is above my talents, and that I approach it with those anxious and awful presentiments which the greatness of the charge and the weakness of my powers so justly inspire." From a man of his talents, this has the odor of false humility. On Jefferson's talents, President Kennedy welcomed America's Nobel laureates at a White House dinner with the observation that "there has never been a greater concentration of intellectual power here at the White House since Jefferson dined alone."

There are some people who by their actions virtually resign from the human race, and I believe their resignations should be accepted.
—JUSTICE JOHN P. BOURCIER

Justice Bourcier was a tough, practical, well-regarded Rhode Island state court judge who believed in long sentences for deserving criminals. I heard him say this in a speech, and wrote it down.

*　*　*

After me, I'm for you.

Representative George Miller told me and Senator Sherrod Brown the story of one politician asking for the help of another in a redistricting struggle, and receiving this answer—a practical political truism if there ever was one.

N ever tease the crocodile until you've crossed the stream.

 —ADVICE TO SENATOR JOHN CHAFEE FROM
  HIS FATHER

A lways let the other fellow have it your way.

 —ADVICE TO SENATOR CLAIBORNE PELL FROM
  HIS FATHER

Two good pieces of practical advice from fathers whose sons became great U.S. senators from Rhode Island.

The judge, even when he is free, is still not wholly free. He is not to innovate at pleasure. He is not a knight-errant, roaming at will in pursuit of his own ideal of beauty or of goodness. He is to draw his inspiration from consecrated principles. He is not to yield to spasmodic sentiment, to vague and unregulated benevolence. He is to exercise a discretion informed by tradition, methodized by analogy, disciplined by system, and subordinated to the "primordial necessity of order in the social life." Wide enough in all conscience is the field of discretion that remains.

—JUSTICE BENJAMIN CARDOZO, *THE NATURE OF THE JUDICIAL PROCESS*

This is the best call to discipline by judicial officers I've ever come across, and from a brilliant and respected source. I've used this, too.

"Realistic" politicians see the public as manipulable. They act on their belief that they can reach it by speaking to its lower motives, its baser instincts, and often they are right. But at the same time another part of human nature is there and alive. That other part can gather force silently, and then suddenly lash out and bowl the "realists" over. The important thing is not the number of people who think what at any given moment, but the relative power, and momentum, of ideas.

—ELIZABETH DREW, *WASHINGTON JOURNAL*

Washington Journal *is an excellent on-scene, blow-by-blow account of the Nixon presidency falling to the Watergate investigation, and the impeachment process that forced the president's resignation. It includes this salutary observation. Sometimes politics can be merely mechanical; sometimes it is subject to animal impulse; and sometimes things so unexpected can happen as to appear nearly magical.*

Cross-examination of a witness is "the greatest legal engine ever invented for the discovery of truth."
> —JOHN HENRY WIGMORE, WIGMORE'S CODE OF EVIDENCE §1367 (3RD EDITION, 1942)

Monopoly is "the most powerful engine ever employed for the suffocation of commerce."
> —THOMAS JEFFERSON, LETTER TO FREDERICK DE THULEMIER 1785

Each is a good phrase on its own; the parallel structure is striking as a tandem.

All rights tend to declare themselves absolute to their logical extreme. Yet all in fact are limited by the neighborhood of principles of policy which are other than those on which the particular right is founded, and which become strong enough to hold their own when a certain point is reached.

—JUSTICE OLIVER WENDELL HOLMES JR.,
HUDSON COUNTY WATER CO. v. McCARTER, 209
U.S. 349, 355 (1908)

What a lovely description of the anatomy of disagreement at the point of conflict between principles—that place where policies and the law are often most vigorously engaged.

There are more instances of the abridgement of the freedom of the people by gradual and silent encroachments of those in power than by violent and sudden usurpations.
—JAMES MADISON

The greatest dangers to liberty lurk in the insidious encroachment by men of zeal—well-meaning but without understanding.
—LOUIS D. BRANDEIS, U.S. CAPITOL, HOUSE SIDE, FIRST FLOOR

Evil isn't an army that besieges a city from outside the walls. It is a native of the city. It is the mutiny of the garrison, the poison in the water, the ashes in the bread.
—CHARLES MORGAN

The true danger is when liberty is nibbled away, for expedience, and by parts.
—EDMUND BURKE

Neither corruption, nor thievery, nor tyranny can announce themselves as such. These wolves must wear sheep's clothing, and inch up on the unsuspecting. The quote from Justice Brandeis is painted inside the United States Capitol, and I noticed it one day walking over to visit a colleague in Congress, Steny Hoyer, and his chief of staff, my friend Terry Lierman.

Extremists, to whatever camp they belong, are the disease germs in the body politic. They can never create, but when the general health of the body is weak, they can bring destruction.

—DUFF COOPER, FROM *TALLEYRAND*

In a novel the author gives some intelligence and a distinguished character to the principal personage; fate takes less trouble: mediocrities play a part in great events simply because they happen to be there.

—TALLEYRAND'S MEMOIRS, REGARDING THE MARQUIS DE LAFAYETTE, QUOTED IN DUFF COOPER'S *TALLEYRAND*

These two observations are related: extremists tend to be mediocrities upraised by events, and they tend to assume a larger role in times when anger and passion inhibit the distinguishing capacity of the public.

A popular Government, without popular information, or the means of acquiring it, is but a Prologue to a Farce or a Tragedy; or perhaps, both. Knowledge will forever govern ignorance: And a people who mean to be their own Governors must arm themselves with the power which knowledge gives.

—WRITINGS OF JAMES MADISON

No more need be said.

* * *

[I]t has happened in all ages of the world that some have labored, and others, without labor, have enjoyed a larger proportion of the fruits. This is wrong, and should not continue. To secure to each laborer the whole product of his labor as nearly as possible is a worthy object of any good government.

—ABRAHAM LINCOLN, FROM HIS SPEECH "THE DEMAND OF LABOR"

There are much greater storms in politics. If it's piracy you want, with broadsides, boarding parties, walking the plank, and blood on the deck, this is the place!

——DAVID LLOYD GEORGE, FORMER PRIME
MINISTER OF ENGLAND

This was the elderly Lloyd George's advice to a young man trying to decide between a career in the Royal Navy and a career in the House of Commons.

Great quarrels . . . arise from small occasions but seldom from small causes.

—Winston Churchill, *The Gathering Storm*

An important point to reckon with when great causes are in opposition: it is wise to avoid presenting even small occasions for the great causes to become great quarrels.

* * *

Neither was there any among them that lacked: for as many as were possessors of lands or houses, sold them, and brought the prices of the things that were sold, and laid them down at the apostles' feet; and distribution was made unto every man according as he had need.

—Acts 4:32–35

Redistribution of wealth in the Bible? Compare the principle, "from each according to his ability, to each according to his need."

I must study the plain physical facts of the case, ascertain what is possible and learn what appears to be wise and right.

—ABRAHAM LINCOLN

If one were to dress the process of political analysis down to the bone, removing everything else but the essential form, it would be hard to do it any better than this—a good example of simplicity in expression, and reduction to bare essence.

Governments can err, presidents do make mistakes, but the immortal Dante tells us that Divine justice weighs the sins of the cold-blooded and the sins of the warm-hearted in different scales. Better the occasional faults of a government that lives in a spirit of charity than the consistent omissions of a government frozen in the ice of its own indifference.

—FRANKLIN D. ROOSEVELT, "A RENDEZVOUS WITH DESTINY," SPEECH BEFORE THE DEMOCRATIC NATIONAL CONVENTION, JUNE 27, 1936, PHILADELPHIA

When so much of government amounts to a contest among powerful interests over spoils and advantage, the "spirit of charity" is a vital touchstone.

And when the last law was down, and the Devil turned 'round on you, where would you hide . . . the laws all being flat? This country is planted thick with laws, from coast to coast, Man's laws, not God's! And if you cut them down . . . do you really think you could stand upright in the winds that would blow then? Yes, I'd give the Devil benefit of law, for my own safety's sake!

——ROBERT BOLT, *A MAN FOR ALL SEASONS*

In this play, a young acolyte suggested to Thomas More that to root out the Devil he'd knock down all the laws of England so as to allow the Devil no shelter amidst the laws. This was More's response. Long-term damage can be done when short-term passions drive expedience and shortcuts. Eyes on the prize; eyes on the prize.

CHAPTER SEVEN

AMERICA

America is not just a land, it's a promise.

—SENATOR EDWARD M. KENNEDY, SPEAKING TO THE
SENATE AFTER CASTING HIS 15,000TH VOTE

For we must consider that we shall be as a city upon a hill. The eyes of all people are upon us . . .
—JOHN WINTHROP, "A MODEL OF CHRISTIAN CHARITY," 1630

The greatest service this country could render to the rest of the world would be to put its own house in order and to make of American civilization an example of decency, humanity, and societal success from which others could derive whatever they might find useful to their own purposes.
—GEORGE F. KENNAN

Bill Clinton echoed these remarks in his 2008 speech at our Convention, saying that America has always impressed the world more "by the power of our example than by the example of our power." I have often used the Winthrop and Clinton quotes. The Winthrop quote is derived from Matthew 5:14, "Ye are the light of the world. A city that is set on a hill cannot be hid," which continues at verse 16: "Let your light so shine before men, that they may see your good works, and glorify your Father which is in heaven."

The energy, the faith, the devotion which we bring to this endeavor will light our country and all who serve it—and the glow from that fire can truly light the world!
—JOHN F. KENNEDY, INAUGURAL ADDRESS, 1961

"Ask not . . ." was not the best line of JFK's speech. This line echoes John Winthrop, and in turn was echoed by President Barack Obama's Inaugural Address: "Those ideals still light the world, and we will not give them up for expedience's sake." The reference in "America the Beautiful" that our "alabaster cities gleam" is not for nothing.

A hurry of hoofs in a village street,

A shape in the moonlight, a bulk in the dark,

And beneath, from the pebbles, in passing, a spark

Struck out by a steed flying fearless and fleet;

That was all! And yet through the gloom and the light,

The fate of a nation was riding that night;

And the spark struck out by that steed, in his flight,

Kindled the land into flame with its heat.

—HENRY WADSWORTH LONGFELLOW,
FROM "PAUL REVERE'S RIDE"

And what a spark it was.

We are justly proud of being descended from men who have set the world an example of founding civil institutions on the great and united principles of human freedom and human knowledge.

No combination of circumstances more favorable to the experiment can ever be expected to occur. The last hopes of mankind, therefore, rest with us; and if it should be proclaimed, that our example had become an argument against the experiment, the knell of popular liberty would be sounded throughout the earth.

—DANIEL WEBSTER, SPEAKING AT BUNKER HILL

I came across this quotation at a time when our example of human freedom and human knowledge was yielding to expedience, and to the power and money of special influence. When these things go wrong in America, it matters more, because we are not just here for covetous grasping at spoils; we are an example to the world, and bear a special responsibility. When we fail, we pay a dual price: our failure, and our diminished example.

* * *

The intensity of the frenzy is the most hopeful feature of this disgraceful exhibition;—of hysterical, unintelligent fear—which is quite foreign to the generous American nature. It will pass like the Know-nothing days, but the sense of shame and sin should endure.

—LOUIS BRANDEIS, LATER SUPREME COURT JUSTICE

This was Louis Brandeis's reaction to the Palmer Raids, targeting undesirables for arrest and deportation, launched by Attorney General Palmer after radical bomb plots were discovered. The Know-Nothing Party briefly controlled the Rhode Island General Assembly in the 1850s during a wave of anti-immigrant, anti-Catholic passion.

. . . Sail on, O Ship of State!

Sail on, O Union, strong and great!

Humanity with all its fears,

With all the hopes of future years,

Is hanging breathless on thy fate.

—LONGFELLOW'S QUOTE, SENT TO WINSTON
CHURCHILL IN LONGHAND BY PRESIDENT FRANKLIN
D. ROOSEVELT IN WORLD WAR II

I was presiding during Senator John Warner's farewell speech, and he saw me reciting these words as he quoted them. He came up afterward onto the podium to talk to me about this poem. He later brought to me a copy of the full poem. He was a wonderful, honorable senator, and very kind to me. He was also a man of great political courage. I miss him in the Senate.

[The American system] has had the advantage of relegating questions not only intricate and delicate, but peculiarly liable to excite political passions, to the cool, dry atmosphere of judicial determination.

—JAMES BRYCE, *THE AMERICAN COMMONWEALTH*

The "cool, dry atmosphere" of judicial determination is a memorable phrase, particularly when political proceedings get hot and steamy—and reflects one of the many brilliant aspects of America's balance of government.

* * *

The jury is pre-eminently a political institution; it must be regarded as one form of the sovereignty of the people.

—ALEXIS DE TOCQUEVILLE, *DEMOCRACY IN AMERICA*,
FROM THE CHAPTER "ON WHAT TEMPERS THE
TYRANNY OF THE MAJORITY"

In America's balance of governmental institutions, the important role of the jury is often overlooked. Not for nothing did the Founders reference the jury three times in the Constitution and Bill of Rights. When the governor is in your enemy's pocket; when the lobbyists have the legislature tied in knots; when the newspaper owner is steering public opinion against you; the hard square corners of the jury box can provide a last sanctuary.

To hold forth a lively experiment that a most flour-
ishing civil state may stand and best be maintained
with full liberty in religious concernments.

—THE ROYAL CHARTER OF 1663 GRANTED BY
KING CHARLES II ESTABLISHING THE COLONY OF
RHODE ISLAND AND PROVIDENCE PLANTATIONS IN
NEW ENGLAND

John Clarke of Newport obtained this charter providing in Rhode Island the world's first formal establishment of freedom of conscience, distinguishing us from the rigid theocracy of Massachusetts, where ideological conformity was enforced at the gallows. This "lively experiment" in Rhode Island forged the path for American freedom of conscience, one of our greatest national blessings. At a time when international trade depended on bonds of trust often forged in religious and ethnic identity, this liberty also allowed trading networks of Quakers, Baptists and Jews to connect in Newport, and created abundant wealth and commerce. This freedom of religion was the great legacy of Rhode Island's founder, Roger Williams.

For happily, the Government of the United States, which gives to bigotry no sanction, to persecution no assistance, requires only that they who live under its protection should demean themselves as good citizens in giving it at all occasions their effectual support.
——George Washington, *Letter to the Congregation of the Touro Synagogue, August 1790*

The letter is a reply to a letter from the synagogue's warden, Moses Seixas, which asked for assurance that it would be the policy of Washington's government to give "to bigotry no sanction, to persecution no assistance." Washington, with the politician's eye for a good phrase, appropriated it and copied it back to the warden in his answer. The Washington letter is still read annually in a ceremony at the Touro Synagogue. And America has more and more honored Washington's promise to Warden Seixas.

* * *

Why stand we here idle? What is it that gentlemen wish? What would they have? Is life so dear, or peace so sweet, as to be purchased at the price of chains and slavery? Forbid it, Almighty God! I know not what course others may take; but as for me, give me liberty or give me death.
——Patrick Henry, 1775

As full-throated a blast of America political speech as I have ever come across. Need to rev up your passion? Just read this. The fire leaps off the page. Evidently, it was just as inspiring in real life as on the cold page. Edward Carrington, listening to this speech through the windows of St. John's Church in Richmond, said "Let me be buried on this spot." In 1810, he was.

Every true man has pride of race, and under appropriate circumstances when the rights of others, his equals before the law, are not to be affected, it is his privilege to express such pride and to take such action based upon it as to him seems proper. But I deny that any legislative body or judicial tribunal may have regard to the race of citizens when the civil rights of those citizens are involved.

—JUSTICE JOHN HARLAN, DISSENTING IN
PLESSY V. FERGUSON

One of the functions of a judicial dissent is to assure future generations that not everyone was victim to the folly and bias of an era. This is from a great dissent to a tragic opinion. Even the United Sates Supreme Court has its moments of disgrace, and the Plessy *decision was one, upholding the fraudulent doctrine of "separate but equal." Harlan's lonely dissent earns the gratitude of history. The phrasing is beautifully lucid, and the distinction is well formed and phrased.*

Three-and-a-half centuries ago the first Negroes arrived at Jamestown. They did not arrive in brave ships in search of a home for freedom. They did not mingle fear and joy, in brave expectation that in this new world anything would be possible to a man strong enough to reach for it. They came in darkness and they came in chains.

—LYNDON B. JOHNSON AT THE SIGNING OF THE VOTING RIGHTS ACT OF 1965

I didn't think of Lyndon Johnson as being a very compelling orator, but this is a wonderful wind-up to the final rhythmic punch.

Four score and seven years ago our fathers brought forth on this continent, a new nation, conceived in liberty, and dedicated to the proposition that all men are created equal.

Now we are engaged in a great civil war, testing whether that nation, or any nation so conceived and so dedicated, can long endure. We are met on a great battlefield of that war. We have come to dedicate a portion of that field, as a final resting place for those who here gave their lives that that nation might live. It is altogether fitting and proper that we do this.

But in a larger sense, we cannot dedicate—we cannot consecrate—we cannot hallow—this ground. The brave men, living and dead, who struggled here, have consecrated it, far above our poor power to add or detract. The world will little note, nor long remember, what we say here, but it can never forget what they did here. It is for us the living, rather, to be here dedicated to the great task remaining before us—that from these honored dead we take increased devotion to that cause for which they gave the last full measure of devotion—that we here highly resolve that these dead shall not have died in vain—that this nation, under God, shall have a new birth of freedom—and that government of the people, by the people, and for the people, shall not perish from the earth.

—ABRAHAM LINCOLN, THE GETTYSBURG ADDRESS

There is nothing to add to this great speech.

I well remember a still higher tribute paid us that day. We were coming on that dreadful field under General Gordon, and we were passing through the open ranks of a superb brigade of infantry. We were ragged and we had no shoes. The banners our army had borne to the heights of Gettysburg were bloody and in shreds. There were less than eight thousand of us with arms in our hands, though they were bright and burnished still. Great divisions, the very names of which had once spread terror in the North, were reduced to small regiments, and regiments to squads. We were only a shadow of an army, a ghost of an army, and as we marched in tattered, hungry columns between those magnificent straight lines of well-fed men, faultlessly armed and perfectly equipped, most of us wished, as our great chief did, that we might have been numbered with the fallen in the last battle. But, as we marched forward with our heads up—no Confederate soldier ever held his head any other way and no Southerner ever should—as we marched forward in the silence of that sodden field, suddenly I heard a sharp order sent down that blue line, and on the instant I saw that whole brigade present arms to us—to us, the survivors of the Army of Northern Virginia. It was a Maine brigade, comrades, and I confess to you that though more than sixty years have passed since that gray April noon, I never hear the name of that state but that I feel a certain swelling pride as I reflect that there was an army good enough to deserve that salute—and another army magnanimous enough to give it!

From a speech written by Douglas Southall Freeman, Pulitzer Prize winning author, for his father to deliver at the 1926 "campfire" of the Confederate Veteran Camp of New York. Naval War College Review XLIV no. 3, seq. 335 (Summer 1991) pp. 75–83. This and the following description of the salute at Appomattox suggest how powerfully a simple gesture, perhaps even

arising from a spontaneous impulse of General Chamberlain, can echo down
history's halls, and what an effect it must have had in binding our sundered
nation back together. This description has brought me to tears.

When the time came to march out and give up our guns and
flags, in surrender, I asked General Gordon to let my brigade——as
it had fired the last shot——to be the last to stack arms. This he read-
ily granted. In a little while my time came. A heavy line of Union
soldiers stood opposite us in absolute silence. As my decimated and
ragged little band with their bullet-torn banner marched to its place,
someone in the blue line broke the silence and called for three cheers
for the last brigade to surrender. It was taken up all about him by
those who knew what it meant. But for us this soldierly generosity
was more than we could bear. Many of the grizzled veterans wept
like women, and my own eyes were as blind as my voice was dumb.
Years have passed since then and time mellows memories, and now
I almost forget the keen agony of that bitter day when I recall how
that line of blue broke its respectful silence to pay such a tribute, at
Appomattox, to the little line in gray that had fought them to the
finish, and only surrendered because it was destroyed.
——Henry Kyd Douglas

I found this latter recollection in my great-uncle Norman Whitridge's
book, Take One At Night. *His Introduction gives very kind thanks to my*
great-aunt Janetta: "In a sense this is her book. At least it is the last thing
we did together, and for that reason I like to think that those to whom I am
giving it, those who knew her and loved her——the two things were almost
synonymous——will find that these passages suggest not just my random choice
but Janetta's very special combination of taste, humor, kindliness and com-
mon sense."

With malice toward none, with charity for all, with firmness in the right as God gives us to see the right, let us strive on to finish the work we are in, to bind up the nation's wounds, to care for him who shall have borne the battle and for his widow and his orphan, to do all which may achieve and cherish a just and lasting peace among ourselves and with all nations.
— President Lincoln's Second Inaugural Address

Your men must keep their houses and their mules. They will need them for the spring ploughing.
— Ulysses S. Grant to Robert E. Lee at the end of the Civil War

Healing words from our greatest president, and his greatest general.

After four years of arduous service, marked by unsurpassed courage and fortitude, the Army of Northern Virginia has been compelled to yield to overwhelming numbers and resources. I need not tell the survivors of so many hard-fought battles, who have remained steadfast to the last, that I have consented to this result from no distrust of them; but feeling that valor and devotion could accomplish nothing that would compensate for the loss that must have attended a continuance of the contest, I determined to avoid the useless sacrifice of those whose past services have endeared them to their countrymen.

By the terms of the Agreement, Officers and men can return to their homes and remain until exchanged. You will take with you the satisfaction, that proceeds from the consciousness of a duty faithfully performed, and I earnestly pray that a merciful God will extend to you his blessing and protection. With unceasing admiration of your constancy and devotion to your Country and a grateful remembrance of your kind and generous consideration of myself, I bid you all an Affectionate Farewell.

—GENERAL LEE'S FAREWELL ADDRESS, APPOMATTOX COURT HOUSE, APRIL 10, 1865

And this is the dignified surrender of the defeated commander, attentive more than anything to the sensibilities of his men.

December 19, 1956—This is a historic week because segregation on buses has now been declared unconstitutional. Within a few days the Supreme Court's Mandate will reach Montgomery and you will be re-boarding integrated buses. This places upon us all a tremendous responsibility of maintaining, in face of what could be some unpleasantness, a calm and loving dignity befitting good citizens and members of our race. If there is violence in word or deed it must not be our people who commit it.

For your help and convenience the following suggestions are made. Will you read, study and memorize them so that our nonviolent determination may not be endangered. First some general suggestions:

1. Not all white people are opposed to integrated buses. Accept goodwill on the part of many.
2. The whole bus is now for the use of all people. Take a vacant seat.
3. Pray for guidance and commit yourself to complete nonviolence in word and action as you enter the bus.
4. Demonstrate the calm dignity of our Montgomery people in your actions.
5. In all things observe ordinary rules of courtesy and good behavior.
6. Remember this is not a victory for Negroes alone, but for all Montgomery and the South. Do not boast! Do not brag!
7. Be quiet but friendly; proud, but not arrogant; joyous, but not boisterous.
8. Be loving enough to absorb evil and understanding enough to turn an enemy into a friend.

NOW FOR SOME SPECIFIC SUGGESTIONS:

1. The bus driver is in charge of the bus and has been instructed to obey the law. Assume that he will cooperate in helping you occupy a vacant seat.

2. Do not deliberately sit by a white person, unless there is no other seat.

3. In sitting down by person, white or colored, say "May I" or 'Pardon me' as you sit. This is a common courtesy.

4. If cursed do not curse back. If pushed, do not push back. If struck, do not strike back, but evidence love and goodwill at all times.

5. In case of an incident, talk as little as possible, and always in a quiet tone. Do not get up from your seat! Report all serious incidents to the bus driver.

6. For the first few days try to get on the bus with a friend in whose nonviolence you have confidence. You can uphold one another by a glance or prayer.

7. If another person is being molested, do not arise and go to his defense, but pray for the oppressor and use moral and spiritual force to carry on the struggle for justice.

8. According to your own ability and personality, do not be afraid to experiment with new and creative techniques for achieving reconciliation and social change.

9. If you feel you cannot take it, walk for another week or two. We have confidence in our people. GOD BLESS YOU ALL.

    —INTEGRATED BUS SUGGESTIONS

The etiquette of transformation: the Montgomery Improvement Association (The Rev. Martin Luther King Jr., president) prepared this leaflet to guide the black population of Montgomery after the successful conclusion of the bus boycott.

Tell them that the sacrifice was not in vain. Tell them that by way of the shop, the field, the skilled hand, habits of thrift and economy, by way of industrial school and college, we are coming. We are crawling up, working up, yea, bursting up. Often through oppression, unjust discrimination, and prejudice, but through them, we are coming up. And with proper habits, intelligence, and property, there is no power on earth that can permanently stay our progress.

—BOOKER T. WASHINGTON

Booker T. Washington spoke at Harvard University's alumni dinner in 1896, and posed himself the question what message there might be from the South to those like Robert Gould Shaw, Civil War commander of the African American Fifty-Fourth Massachusetts Infantry, "who Harvard offered up on death's altar." This was his answer.

The spirit of liberty is the spirit which is not too sure that it is right; the spirit of liberty is the spirit which seeks to understand the minds of other men and women; the spirit of liberty is the spirit which weights their interests alongside its own without bias; the spirit of liberty remembers that not even a sparrow falls to earth unheeded.

—JUDGE LEARNED HAND, "THE SPIRIT OF LIBERTY," 1944

When patriotism is used to divide Americans and stampede public opinion, it is good to remember that these wise and gentle words were delivered on "I Am an American Day" in wartime.

A senator of the United States is an ambulant converging point for pressures and counter-pressures of high, medium and low purposes.

—WILLIAM S. WHITE, *CITADEL,* P. 135

A description I have found to be true, and never better said.

A United States senator is a constitutional impediment to the smooth and orderly functioning of staff.
——SENATOR TOM HARKIN

This mildly ironic observation reflects the sometimes prominent role of staff in legislative decision making.

L et us not assassinate this lad further, Senator. You have done enough. Have you no sense of decency, sir, at long last? Have you left no sense of decency?

—ATTORNEY JOSEPH WELCH, TO SENATOR JOSEPH MCCARTHY, SENATE PERMANENT SUBCOMMITTEE ON INVESTIGATIONS DURING ARMY-MCCARTHY HEARINGS

This scene was captured by the television cameras of the day, and can be seen in the film, Point of Order. It is worth seeing. Very often, political outcomes are determined by the weight of contesting forces vying for power. This private lawyer's sincere, direct outrage at an attack on his young associate punctured the thrall woven by Senator McCarthy from the fears and passions of the time. Mere words, from a Boston lawyer who had just had enough, turned the tide of history. This stands with Joshua Chamberlain's salute at Appomattox as a time when unexpected words made a great difference.

The underlying strength of a nation that can get more ingloriously mixed up than any other and somehow gloriously come out of it in the end.

—JAMES THURBER, *ALARMS AND DIVERSIONS*, P. 121

You can always count on Americans to do the right thing—after they've tried everything else.

—WINSTON CHURCHILL

CHAPTER EIGHT

CALLING, FAITH, AND SERVICE

God is just . . . [and] his justice cannot sleep forever.

—THOMAS JEFFERSON, ON SLAVERY

The Lord bless you and keep you; the Lord make his face to shine upon you and be gracious unto you; the Lord lift up his countenance upon you and give you peace.

—*BOOK OF COMMON PRAYER: THE COMMITTAL PRAYER*

As blessings go, this is as good as it gets: evocative, simple, and strong.

I'll be around in the dark; I'll be everywhere, wherever you can look. Wherever there is a fight so hungry people can eat, I'll be there. Wherever there's a cop beating up a guy, I'll be there. I'll be there in the way guys yell when they're mad. I'll be there in the way kids laugh when they're hungry and they know supper's ready. When people are eatin' the stuff they raised, and livin' in the houses they built, I'll be there, too.

—JOHN STEINBECK, *THE GRAPES OF WRATH*, AS
DELIVERED BY HENRY FONDA PLAYING TOM JOAD
IN THE MOVIE ADAPTATION

Tom Joad's farewell to his mother may be the most stirring passage in any American film. Henry Fonda delivers it beautifully. You know what's coming, and this gives it meaning that is both deeply Christian and touchingly human, both ethereal and immediate.

It is not up to us to complete the work, but neither are we free to desist from it.
>—Rabbi Tarfon

The arc of a moral universe is long, but it bends toward justice.
>—Martin Luther King Jr.

The strongest and sweetest songs yet remain to be sung.
>—Walt Whitman, last line of *Leaves of Grass*

Ask, and it shall be given;
Seek, and ye shall find;
Knock and it shall be opened unto you.
>—Matthew 7:7–8

Patience and confidence are a strong combination.

Field and forest, vale and mountain,

Flowering meadow, flashing sea,

Chanting bird and flowing fountain,

Call us to rejoice in Thee.

——HYMN: "JOYFUL, JOYFUL, WE ADORE THEE"
HENRY VAN DYKE

My wife Sandra finds God's joy in nature, particularly in the flashing sea, and selected this hymn for our wedding.

All shall be well, and all manner of things shall be well.

—Juliana of Norwich

Grant, O Lord,
That in all the joys of life
We may never forget to be kind.
Help us to be unselfish with friendship,
Thoughtful of those less happy than ourselves,
And eager to bear the burdens of others;
Through Jesus Christ, our Savior. Amen.
—St. Paul's School Prayer

Go forth into the world in peace; be of good courage; hold fast to that which is good; render no one evil for evil; strengthen the faint-hearted; support the weak; help the afflicted; honor all people; love and serve the Lord, rejoicing in the Power of the Holy Spirit.
—Book of Common Prayer

"Hold fast to that which is good," spoken by St. Paul in 1 Thessalonians 5:21, is the SPS school motto. I am deeply ambivalent about my time at St. Paul's School, but for better or for worse, it was the single place I had lived the longest, until I was nearly thirty-five years old, when our home in Providence took over. Over my years at that boarding school, hymns and liturgy were pounded into me, and since have become consistent and often comforting resources.

Once to every man and nation,
    comes the moment to decide,
in the strife of truth with falsehood,
    for the good or evil side;
some great cause, some great decision,
    offering each the bloom or blight,
and the choice goes by forever,
    'twixt that darkness and that light.
....

Though the cause of evil prosper,
    yet the truth alone is strong;
Though her portion be the scaffold,
    and upon the throne be wrong;
Yet that scaffold sways the future,
    and behind the dim unknown,
Standeth God within the shadow,
    keeping watch above his own.
           —HYMN: "ONCE TO EVERY MAN AND NATION"
           JAMES RUSSELL LOWELL, 1849

Also sometimes:

Truth forever on the scaffold,
Wrong forever on the throne,
Yet that scaffold sways the future
And behind the dim unknown
Standeth God within the shadow
Keeping watch above his own.

I first heard this hymn as a 60-something-pound eleven-year-old, thousands of miles away from my family in what seemed the vast cavern of the St. Paul's School Chapel. The hymn was slightly terrifying, with its ponderous swaying measure and ominous imagery. Beneath all that, there's actually the kernel of a positive message. It was a regular hymn of the school, and always conveyed to me a sense of consequence and gloom. Later in the hymn comes the couplet: "Then it is the brave man chooses while the coward stands aside, till the multitude make virtue of the faith they had denied."

This is the true joy in life . . . being used for a purpose recognized by yourself as a mighty one . . . being a force of nature instead of a feverish selfish little clod of ailments and grievances.

——George Bernard Shaw

Both sides of this comparison are wonderfully phrased. To feel useful toward a mighty purpose is indeed a joy. And do we not all know someone so self-absorbed as to have become a "feverish selfish little clod of ailments and grievances"? What a contrast between the blessing of one and the tragedy of the other, as destinies for the human soul.

Agnus Dei qui tollis peccata mundi, Miserere nobis
Agnus Dei qui tollis peccata mundi, Miserere nobis
Agnus Dei qui tollis peccata mundi, dona eis requiem
  sempiternam.
  —LAMB OF GOD

As a Rhode Island public official I go quite often to Catholic funerals and masses. Even in Latin, I find these words simple, moving, and beautiful. I have heard them sung so beautifully as to bring tears to my eyes.

Bring me my Cross of burning gold;

Bring me my Arrows of desire:

Bring me my Spear: O Clouds unfold!

Bring me my Chariot of fire!

I will not cease from Mental Fight,

Nor shall my Sword sleep in my hand:

Till we have built Jerusalem

In [this our] green and pleasant land.

—WILLIAM BLAKE, "AND DID THOSE FEET IN
ANCIENT TIME"

I put this verse, thus edited, on the plaque in front of the attorney general's office when I was attorney general of Rhode Island. People in public service should never let their swords sleep in their hands when there are wrongs to be righted or rights to be defended.

Lord, now lettest thou thy servant depart in peace, according to
thy word;
For mine eyes have seen thy salvation, which thou hast prepared
before the face of all people.
—THE *"NUNC DIMITTIS"*

*These words are attributed to Simeon, a devout believer in the coming
Savior, when he was presented with the infant Jesus and saw that his prayers
and faith were answered. In a nutshell: "I can now die happy." My father, a
Marine Corps dive bomber pilot in World War II, reported that he found this
verse comforting as he rolled his Dauntless dive bomber over and down into
its dives "so steep that you hung in the shoulder harness" as the dive brakes
held the plane. His greatest anxiety was not the dive-bombing runs, but the
navigation across the vast Pacific to tiny specks of island; great was the relief
when, as fuel ran low, his tiny destination came into sight!*

DO IT ANYWAY
People are often unreasonable, illogical and self-centered;
Forgive them anyway.
If you are kind, people may accuse you of selfish ulterior motives;
Be kind anyway.
If you are successful, you will win some false friends and true
    enemies;
Succeed anyway.
If you are honest and frank, people may cheat you;
Be honest and frank anyway.
What you spend years building may be destroyed overnight;
Build anyway.
If you find serenity and happiness, others may be jealous;
Be happy anyway.
The good you do today people will often forget tomorrow;
Do good anyway.
Give the world the best you have, and it may never be enough;
Give the world the best you've got anyway.
You see, in the final analysis, it is between you and God;
It was never between you and them anyway.
             —ATTRIBUTED TO MOTHER TERESA

Life presents the constant temptation to model your conduct on the conduct of others, rather than on your own standards for yourself. Yielding to those temptations, even when satisfying in the moment, is too often cause for regret.

I have fought the good fight, I have finished the race, I have kept the faith.

—2 Timothy 4:7

Familiar to everyone, but still simple and powerful.

CHAPTER NINE

MISTAKES, DEFEAT, AND FAILURE

The world breaks everyone, and afterward some
are strong at the broken places.

——Ernest Hemingway

Try again; fail again, but fail better.

—SAMUEL BECKETT

All that is gold does not glitter,
Not all those who wander are lost;
The old that was strong does not wither,
Deep roots are not reached by the frost.
From the fire a flame shall be woken,
A light from the shadows shall spring;
Renewed be the blade that was broken,
The crownless again shall be King.

—J. R. R. TOLKIEN

This verse was sent to me by a thoughtful friend after a defeat that I took very hard. This kind gesture was a real consolation.

H e jests at scars, that never felt a wound.
—SHAKESPEARE, *ROMEO AND JULIET*

One jests less at the scars of others after feeling a few wounds oneself.

Our landings in the Cherbourg-Havre area have failed to gain a satisfactory foothold and I have withdrawn the troops. My decision to attack at this time and place was based on the best information available. The troops, the air and the Navy did all that bravery and devotion to duty could do. If any blame or fault attaches to the attempt it is mine alone.

—NOTE PREPARED IN ADVANCE OF D-DAY (JUNE 6, 1944) BY GENERAL DWIGHT EISENHOWER, TO BE READ IN THE EVENT OF FAILURE

He did not need to use it, but this is a very gracious acceptance of responsibility, prepared in the event of failure. It's also a reminder of what an uncertain gamble the D-Day invasion was at the time. Imagine Eisenhower's thoughts as he wrote this.

* * *

I went out to Charing-Cross to see Major General Harrison hanged, drawn and quartered—which was done there—he looking cheerfully as any man could do in that condition. He was presently cut down and his head and heart shown to the people, at which there was great shouts of joy.

—FROM THE DIARY OF SAMUEL PEPYS FOR OCTOBER 1, 1660

Chin up. Could be a lot worse.

Sweet are the uses of adversity.
  —SHAKESPEARE, *As You Like It*

Man must suffer to be wise.
  —AESCHYLUS, *Agamemnon*

It is the rule of God's providence that we should succeed by
failure.
  —JOHN HENRY CARDINAL NEWMAN, FROM ARNOLD
      WHITRIDGE'S *Take One At Night*

Man is born broken. He lives by mending. The grace of God is
the glue.
  —EUGENE O'NEILL

*These aphorisms remind us that losses and defeats are often the custodians
of wisdom, sympathy, resilience, and renewal. Who we are is more often than
not determined by how we respond to adversity. And maintaining good morale
in hard circumstances is a special kind of courage.*

For now I see the true old times are dead,
When every morning brought a noble chance,
And every chance brought out a noble knight;*
And I, the last, go forth companionless.
And the days darken around me, and the years,
Among new men, strange faces, other minds.
—Tennyson, "Morte d'Arthur"

Churchill's version:

When every morn brought forth a noble chance
And every chance brought forth a noble knight.

Churchill can improve on anything! But the haunting image is not the one Churchill improved, it is the lonely soul's going companionless, into dark days and years filled with strange faces.

It is common sense to take a method and try it. If it fails, admit it frankly and try another. But above all, try something.
—Franklin D. Roosevelt

Take risks. Ask big questions. Don't be afraid to make mistakes. If you don't make mistakes, you're not reaching far enough.
—David Packard, founder of Hewlett-Packard

The most painful thing to experience is not defeat but regret.
—Leo Buscaglia

I know I'm going to make mistakes. I just want them to be new ones.
—Ric Ohrstrom, on a phone call

Rock bottom is a very good foundation to build on.
—Carl Wagner, Edward Kennedy's 1980 field director

Hey, you know what? Whenever I fall, I make it into a move.
—My son, Alexander, age 6, on dancing (and life)

I think no further explanation here is required.

By deep knowledge of principle, one can change disturbance into order, change danger into safety, change destruction into survival, change calamity into fortune.

—TAO, *THE BOOK OF BALANCE AND HARMONY*

And the corollary is that by misunderstanding, one's intervention can make more disturbance, danger, destruction and calamity. As my press secretary in the attorney general's office, Jim Martin, used to observe, "You can always make it worse."

CHAPTER TEN

PEACE AT THE LAST

Now the laborer's task is o'er;

Now the battle day is past . . .

Father, in Thy gracious keeping

Leave we now thy servant sleeping.

—JOHN ELLERTON'S HYMN READ AT
PRESIDENT FRANKLIN D. ROOSEVELT'S FUNERAL

O Lord, support us all the days long of this troublous life,

Until the shadows lengthen,

And the evening comes,

And the busy world is hushed,

And the fever of life is over.

Then in thy mercy grant us a safe lodging,

And a holy rest, and peace at the last.

Amen.

—ATTRIBUTED TO JOHN HENRY CARDINAL NEWMAN

This was my father's favorite prayer, and was read at his funeral. Death is so gently described here. The American Pacific War Memorial in Manila has an abridged version of this prayer inscribed on its chapel wall.

"Have you news of my boy Jack?"
Not this tide.
"When d'you think that he'll come back?"
Not with this wind blowing, and this tide.
"Has anyone else had word of him?"
Not this tide.
For what is sunk will hardly swim,
Not with this wind blowing, and this tide.
"Oh, dear, what comfort can I find?"
None this tide,
Nor any tide,
Except he did not shame his kind—
Not even with that wind blowing, and that tide.
Then hold your head up all the more,
This tide,
And every tide;
Because he was the son you bore,
And gave to that wind blowing and that tide.

—AFTER LONG UNCERTAINTY AND WHILE JACK WAS
LISTED MISSING IN ACTION, RUDYARD KIPLING WROTE
THIS ABOUT HIS SON KILLED AT EIGHTEEN IN THE
TRENCHES OF WORLD WAR I.

If I should die, think only this of me:
That there's some corner of a foreign field
That is forever England. There shall be
In that rich earth a richer dust concealed;
A dust whom England bore, shaped, made aware,
Gave, once, her flowers to love, her ways to roam,
A body of England's, breathing English air,
Washed by the rivers, blest by suns of home.
      —RUPERT BROOKE, "THE SOLDIER"

In Flanders fields the poppies blow
Between the crosses, row on row,
That mark our place; and in the sky
The larks, still bravely singing, fly
Scarce heard among the guns below.
We are the Dead. Short days ago
We lived, felt dawn, saw sunset glow,
Loved and were loved, and now we lie
In Flanders fields.
Take up our quarrel with the foe!
To you from failing hands we throw
The torch—be yours to hold it high!
If ye break faith with us who die
We shall not sleep, though poppies grow
In Flanders fields.

—JOHN D. McCRAE, "IN FLANDERS FIELDS"

They shall grow not old, as we that are left grow old:
Age shall not weary them, nor the years contemn.
At the going down of the sun and in the morning
We will remember them.
—LAURENCE BINYON, "FOR THE FALLEN" 1914

The bloody massacres of World War I stripped entire nations of a generation of men, leaving a generation of women without enough surviving men to marry. The noble hopes of young soldiers sacrificed in muddy trenches left haunting poetry. It is hard to imagine the bloodshed: 21,000 British soldiers were killed or mortally wounded on July 1, 1916, the first day of the Battle of the Somme; on August 2, 1914, the French suffered 27,000 soldiers killed. A British officer who lost 500 men in the July 1st massacres wrote two months later that he "never had a moment's peace since" and shot himself.

L ove bears all things, believes in all things, hopes all things, endures all things.

—1 CORINTHIANS 13:7

At the funeral of a girl who died far too young, the minister recited this verse, and reminded us, "Loss is the shadow side of love."

Lord of all hopefulness, Lord of all joy,
Whose trust, ever child-like, no cares could destroy,
Be there at our waking, and give us, we pray,
Your bliss in our hearts, Lord, at the break of the day.

Lord of all eagerness, Lord of all faith,
Whose strong hands were skilled at the plane and the lathe,
Be there at our labours, and give us, we pray,
Your strength in our hearts, Lord, at the noon of the day.

Lord of all kindliness, Lord of all grace,
Your hands swift to welcome, your arms to embrace,
Be there at our homing, and give us, we pray,
Your love in our hearts, Lord, at the eve of the day.

Lord of all gentleness, Lord of all calm,
Whose voice is contentment, whose presence is balm,
Be there at our sleeping, and give us, we pray,
Your peace in our hearts, Lord, at the end of the day.
　　　—HYMN: "LORD OF ALL HOPEFULNESS,"
　　　JAN STRUTHER

The seasons of life—our waking, our labors, our homing, and our sleeping —are so gently reflected in these stanzas, in clear, kind, simple words.

Vex not his ghost. O, let him pass. He hates him much that would upon the rack of this tough world stretch him out longer.
——SHAKESPEARE, *KING LEAR*

A dying man needs to die, as a sleepy man needs to sleep, and there comes a time when it is wrong, as well as useless, to resist.
——STEWART ALSOP

When a loved one is dying, it can be very hard to let go. These words, by our greatest writer and from a dying man, remind us that there comes a time when the kindest thing can be to let go.

A servant in Baghdad rushed back to his master's house terrified, having seen Death in the marketplace. He begged his master to borrow his horse, to ride away to Samarra. The master loaned his servant his horse, and then went himself into the marketplace. There he saw Death, and asked him, "Why did you terrify my servant this morning?" Death answered him, "I did not mean to terrify your servant. I was just surprised to see him here, as I have an appointment with him this evening in Samarra."
　　—ATTRIBUTED TO SOMERSET MAUGHAM

* * *

We will not weep, though spring be past,
And autumn shadows fall.
These years shall be, although the last,
The loveliest of all.
　　—DUFF COOPER, TO HIS WIFE DIANA

More about love than death, but the consciousness of loss and death is so great that it has a funerary feel.

I have a feeling here of dying fires,
A sense of much and deep unworded censure,
Which, compassing about my private life,
Makes all my public service lustreless
In my own eyes.——I fear I am much condemned
. . . .
Smiling I'd pass to my long home to-morrow
Could I with honour, and my country's gain.
>   ——THOMAS HARDY, WORDS OF LORD NELSON
>   BEFORE TRAFALGAR

Nelson, the great naval hero, carried on a very public affair with Sir William Hamilton's wife, Emma, while commanding the British fleet in Naples. The affair, apparently known to and approved of by Hamilton, produced a daughter and considerable scandal. Nelson's checkered reputation was wiped clean by his sacrifice during his great victory at Trafalgar, a victory which put to rest forever Napoleon's threat to England's shores.

The day is done, and the darkness

Falls from the wings of Night,

As a feather is wafted downward

From an eagle in his flight,

I see the lights of the village

Gleam through the rain and the mist,

And a feeling of sadness comes o'er me

That my soul cannot resist.

A feeling of sadness and longing,

That is not akin to pain,

And resembles sorrow only

As the mist resembles the rain.

—Henry Wadsworth Longfellow, from
"The Day Is Done"

Oh, God, our help in ages past,
Our hope for years to come,
Our shelter from the stormy blast
And our eternal home.

A thousand ages in Thy sight
Are like an evening gone,
Short as the watch that ends the night
Before the rising sun.

Time, like an ever rolling stream,
Bears all its sons away.
They fly forgotten as a dream
Dies at the opening day.

Oh, God, our help in ages past,
Our hope for years to come,
Be Thou our guard while troubles last
And our eternal home.

—Hymn: "Our God, Our Help in Ages Past,"
Issac Watts

This is a hymn that I find very hard to get through without emotion. The images of life and death and shelter touch a chord.

The memories of the blissful moments I have spent with you come creeping over me, and I feel most gratified to God and to you that I have enjoyed them so long. And hard it is for me to give them up and burn to ashes the hopes of future years, when God willing, we might still have lived and loved together and seen our sons grow up to honorable manhood around us. I have, I know, but few and small claims upon Divine Providence, but something whispers to me—perhaps it is the wafted prayer of my little Edgar—that I shall return to my loved ones unharmed. If I do not, my dear Sarah, never forget how much I love you, and when my last breath escapes me on the battlefield, it will whisper your name.

Forgive my many faults, and the many pains I have caused you. How thoughtless and foolish I have often been! How gladly would I wash out with my tears every little spot upon your happiness, and struggle with all the misfortune of this world, to shield you and my children from harm. But I cannot. I must watch you from the spirit land and hover near you, while you buffet the storms with your precious little freight, and wait with sad patience till we meet to part no more.

But, O Sarah! If the dead can come back to this earth and flit unseen around those they loved, I shall always be near you; in the gladdest days and in the darkest nights—amidst your happiest scenes and gloomiest hours—always, always; and if there be a soft breeze upon your cheek, it shall be my breath; or the cool air fans your throbbing temple, it shall be my spirit passing by.

Sarah, do not mourn me dead; think I am gone and wait for me, for we shall meet again.

——PART OF A LETTER FROM SULLIVAN BALLOU,
RHODE ISLANDER AND BROWN UNIVERSITY
GRADUATE, TO HIS WIFE SARAH, WRITTEN
BEFORE HE WAS KILLED AT BULL RUN.

This letter was featured in Ken Burns' excellent series, The Civil War. *The letter so moved him that he carried a copy of it folded in his wallet for twenty-five years.*

O, better that her shattered hulk

Should sink beneath the wave;

Her thunders shook the mighty deep,

And there should be her grave;

Nail to the mast her holy flag,

Set every threadbare sail,

And give her to the god of storms,

The lightning and the gale!

—OLIVER WENDELL HOLMES SR.,
FROM "OLD IRONSIDES"

Dear Madame,

I have been shown in the files of the War Department a statement of the Adjutant General of Massachusetts that you are the mother of five sons who have died gloriously on the field of battle. I feel how weak and fruitless must be any words of mine which should attempt to beguile you from the grief of a loss so overwhelming, but I cannot refrain from tendering to you the consolation that may be found in the thanks of the Republic that they died to save. I pray that the Heavenly Father may assuage the anguish of your bereavement, and leave you only with the cherished memory of the loved and lost, and the solemn pride that must be yours at having laid so costly a sacrifice upon the altar of freedom.

Yours very sincerely and respectfully,

Abraham Lincoln

The recipient of this letter was Mrs. Lydia Bixby of Boston. Happily, it turned out that only two of her sons were killed; two were captured, and one had gone AWOL. The latter three appear to have survived the war. I have to write condolence letters from time to time; this is a great letter.

To lose the earth you know, for greater knowing; to lose the life you have for greater life; to leave the friends you loved, for greater loving; to find a land more kind than home, more large than earth—whereon the pillars of this earth are founded, toward which the conscience of the world is tending—a wind is rising and the rivers flow.
—THOMAS WOLFE, *YOU CAN'T GO HOME AGAIN*

I read this at my father's funeral, to close his eulogy.

LAST WORDS

My work is done. Why wait?
—SUICIDE NOTE LEFT BY GEORGE EASTMAN
(EASTMAN KODAK)

This wallpaper is killing me; one of us has got to go.
—OSCAR WILDE

It is a far, far better thing that I do, than I have ever done; it is a far, far better rest that I go to, than I have ever known.
—CHARLES DICKENS IN *A TALE OF TWO CITIES* BY HIS
CHARACTER SIDNEY CARTON ON THE STEPS TO THE
GUILLOTINE

Now is not the time to make enemies.
—VOLTAIRE, ADVISED TO RENOUNCE THE DEVIL

Let's roll.
—TODD BEAMER, PASSENGER WHO RESISTED
THE HIJACKERS OF UNITED FLIGHT 93 ON
SEPTEMBER 11, 2001

Doctor, I die hard, but I am not afraid to go.
—GEORGE WASHINGTON

Let us cross over the river and rest in the shade of the trees.
—STONEWALL JACKSON